Epochs of Church History

EDITED BY THE

REV. MANDELL CREIGHTON, M.A.

HILDEBRAND AND HIS TIMES

HILDEBRAND

AND HIS TIMES

BY

W. R. W. STEPHENS, M.A,

PREBENDARY OF CHICHESTER AND RECTOR OF WOOLBEDING, SUSSEX
AUTHOR OF 'LIFE OF S. JOHN CHRYSOSTOM' ETC.

Eugene, Oregon

Wipf and Stock Publishers
199 W 8th Ave, Suite 3
Eugene, OR 97401

Hildebrand and His Times
By Stephens, W.R.W.
ISBN: 1-59244-864-X
Publication date 9/14/2004
Previously published by Anson, D.F. Randolph and Co., 1898

PREFACE.

THE period with which this volume deals, including nearly the whole of the eleventh century, and the first twenty years of the twelfth, was an age fruitful of great men and great achievements. The emperor Henry III. of Germany, and his unhappy son Henry IV.; William duke of Normandy, the conqueror of England; Robert Wiscard and his brother Roger, the conquerors of Apulia and Sicily; the countess Matilda of Tuscany, the popes Leo IX., Urban II., Calixtus II., and Hildebrand himself, are only some of the most conspicuous amongst a crowd of persons who were gifted with no common powers. It was an age of movements, and enterprises which did much to shape the future destinies of Europe. It saw the conquest of England by the Normans, and of Southern Italy and Sicily by the same adventurous race; the gradual repulsion of the Saracen from the coasts of Europe, and the first direct aggression upon his conquests in the East. It was marked by the beginnings of scholastic philosophy under Berengar, Lanfranc, and Anselm, and of a more systematic study of law under Burchard of Worms, Ivo of Chartres, and Irnerius of Bologna; it witnessed the rise of a new monastic order, the growth of a new style in architecture, fresh developments in language and literature, a considerable advance in the importance of the middle classes, especially in Germany and Italy, and of the towns as centres of trade.

But incomparably the most wonderful and momentous change effected during this period was the uplifting of the Papacy from the profound degradation into which it had sunk during the ninth century, and had again relapsed, after a brief revival, in the end of the tenth century and the beginning of the eleventh. The reformation begun by the German emperor Henry III. in alliance with the popes whom he nominated was carried forward and almost completed by the genius of Hildebrand. But the elevation of the Papacy brought it at last into collision with the very power by which it had been originally rescued from abasement—the power of the emperor. Which of the two potentates, the temporal or the spiritual head of Christendom, was to be supreme? As the old Carolingian Empire was breaking up more and more into kingdoms, duchies, principalities of various kinds, shaped partly by influences of nationality, partly by the working of the feudal system, what was to be the condition of the Church? Was the Church to follow these divisions, and to become subject to the control of national sovereigns, or feudal suzerains who were often ignorant and brutal petty tyrants? Was she to become national and local in character, with corresponding variations in customs, institutions, ritual, and in time probably in standards both of doctrine and morals; or was the essential unity and catholicity of the Church to be maintained under the sway and direction of one supreme central power? In the mind of Hildebrand there was, and could be, but one answer to these questions. As in the individual, so in the body politic, the spiritual element was clearly designed to command. And where should the supreme spiritual authority of Christendom be vested if not in him who was at once bishop of the old seat of empire and successor of the chief of the apostles? Rome must still be the mistress of the world, but in a higher, deeper, grander sense under the successors of St. Peter than ever she had been under the successors of Augustus. This was the ideal for which Hildebrand strove. The struggle was full of tragical incidents, in which good and evil, base and noble elements were often strangely blended; but that the aim of Hildebrand was a righteous one few will now venture to dispute.

The story of the contest as traced in the following pages is necessarily little more than an outline, but it will serve a good purpose if it in any measure helps and encourages the student to investigate more fully for himself a period which is rich in interest, and in lessons not without their meaning and value for this and all future time.

As notes and references are not admitted into the body of the work, a list of the authorities upon which I have principally relied is here given, chiefly for the benefit of those who may wish to follow out the history of the period for themselves.

I. *Original records, for the most part contemporary with the events.*

Life of Leo IX., by Wibert, his chaplain, in Muratori, III., part i.
Life of Leo IX., by Bruno of Segni, in Muratori, III., part ii.
Annales Romani, in 'Monumenta Germaniæ Historica,' ed. Pertz, vol. v.
Peter Damiani's *Works*, 4 vols. in 2, quarto.
Donizo, *Life of the Countess Matilda*, 'Mon. Germ.,' Pertz, xii.
Lambert of Hersfeld, *Chronicle*: an invaluble record of events from 1073–7, Pertz, v.; but it can be obtained in a separate form.
Adam of Bremen, *Chronicle*, Pertz, vii.; chiefly useful for affairs of North Germany, especially life of archbishop Adalbert.
Annals of Augsburg, Pertz, iii.
Bruno *de Bello Saxonico*, Pertz, v.
Carmen de Bello Saxonico, ed. Waitz.
Humbert, Cardinal, *Treatise against Simony*, Martene and Durand, 'Thesaurus Novus,' vol. v.
Vita Henrici IV., anonymous, Pertz, xii.
Wido of Ferrara, *De Schismate Hildebrandi*, Pertz, xii. Wido was first a Hildebrandist, and afterwards a partisan of Wibert the anti-pope.
Hesso of Strasburg's *Account of the Council of Reims*, A.D. 1119, Pertz, xii.
William of Malmesbury, *Gesta Pontificum* and *Gesta Regum*.
Ordericus Vitalis.

PREFACE ix

- Most important for the affairs of Southern Italy and Sicily:—
Amatus of Salerno, *History of the Norman Conquests in Lower Italy*: it exists, unfortunately, only in a French translation of the thirteenth or fourteenth century. William of Apulia, *Gesta Roberti* (Wiscard), Pertz, xi. Geoffrey Malaterra, Muratori, V. *Chronicle of Monte Cassino*, Pertz, vii.
- For the affairs of Northern Italy:—Arnulf and Landulf, Pertz, viii. Bonitho, bishop of Sutri, *Liber ad amicum*, printed at end of ' Monumenta Gregoriana,' ed. Jaffé.
- For the life of Hildebrand, biographies in Muratori, III., his letters in ' Monumenta Gregoriana,' ed. Jaffé, and *Regesta Pontificum*, vol. i. (ed. Jaffé), a collection of original records of the acts of the popes of great value for the whole history of the period. Benzo, bishop of Alba, ' *Ad Henricum IV.*,' a bitter antagonist of Hildebrand, Pertz, xi.
- Mansi, *Concilia*. The most important passages of these authorities are to be found quoted in Watterich, *Vitæ Pontificum*.

II. *Modern works.*

- J. Voigt, *Hildebrand als Papst Gregorius VII., &c.*, originally published in 1815, the first attempt to form a sound, dispassionate historical estimate of Hildebrand's character and work.
- Floto, *Kaiser Heinrich der Vierte*, 1855: full of useful and interesting matter, but written too much in the spirit of a partisan of Henry IV.
- Gfrörer, *Papst Gregorius VII.*, in 7 vols.: a learned and laborious work, but far too discursive, 1859-61.
- Bowden, *The Life and Pontificate of Gregory VII.*, by John William Bowden, 2 vols., 1840: conscientious and accurate.
- Villemain, *Histoire de Grégoire VII.*, 2 vols., Paris, 1873.
- Milman, *History of Latin Christianity*, vols. iii. and iv. He relies very much upon Floto and Stenzel, and writers more favourable to Henry IV. than to Gregory.
- Montalembert, *Monks of the West*, vols. vi. and vii.
- Sir James Stephen, article on *Hildebrand*, in 'Essays in Ecclesiastical Biography.'

Mignet, *La Lutte des Papes contre les Empereurs*.

Giesbrecht, *Geschichte der Deutschen Kaiserzeit*: a very thorough work of great research, with a full account of all the sources from which it is derived, Leipzig, 1876.

Martens, *Die Besetzung des Päpstlichen Stuhls unter den Kaisern Heinrich III. und IV.*, A.D. 1887.

I could not get this book early enough to make so much use of it as I could have wished. It contains extracts from the chronicles relating to the appointment of the several popes arranged in parallel columns, with critical remarks subjoined.

W. S. Lilly, *Chapters in European History*, 1886. The second chapter in vol. i. is devoted to a sketch of Hildebrand's life, and a careful estimate of his character and of the results of his work.

Every student of the history of the Papacy and the Empire will read and re-read 'The Holy Roman Empire,' by Professor Bryce; and references to Hildebrand in Professor Freeman's works are of course extremely instructive.

The description of Canossa in Chapter XII. is derived chiefly from observations and notes which I made on the spot in May 1886.

W. R. W. STEPHENS.

WOOLBEDING RECTORY:
   January 31, 1888.

CONTENTS.

CHAPTER I.

INTRODUCTORY.

                                                                                             PAGE

Origin of the connexion between the Papacy and transalpine sovereigns—The corruption of the Papacy after the dissolution of the Carolingian Empire—The revival under Otto the Great—The relapse after the death of Otto III. . . 1

CHAPTER II.

Degradation of the Papacy—Beginning of a reformation under Henry III.—The rise of Hildebrand, 1033-47 . . . 14

CHAPTER III.

Progress of the reforming movement—The pontificate of Leo IX., 1047-54. 23

CHAPTER IV.

The death of Henry III.—Pontificates of Victor II. and Stephen IX.—Irregular election of Benedict X.—Election of Nicolas II.—Designs of Hildebrand, 1054-59 38

CHAPTER V.

Pontificate of Nicolas II.—Decree respecting method of election to the Papacy—Alliance with the Normans—Degradation of Benedict X.—Election of Alexander II.—Cadalus of Parma elected anti-pope, 1059-62 46

CHAPTER VI.

Relation of Germany to the Papacy during the minority of Henry IV., 1056-66 59

CHAPTER VII.

The first six years of the reign of Henry IV., 1066-72 . . 69

CHAPTER VIII.

State of the Church in Italy—Survey of the position of the Papacy in Europe—Death of Alexander II., 1073 . . 77

CHAPTER IX.

Hildebrand elected pope—First two years of his pontificate, 1073-75 89

CHAPTER X.

Revolt of the Saxons—Beginning of the strife between Henry IV. and Gregory VII., 1073-76 102

CHAPTER XI.

Deposition of Gregory VII. by the Council of Worms—Henry IV. excommunicated at Rome by the pope—Diet of Tribur and suspension of the king's authority—Henry escapes from Speier and goes to Italy, January 1076—January 1077 . 115

CHAPTER XII.

Meeting between Henry and the pope at Canossa—Results of the meeting—Diet of Forcheim—Election of Rudolf of Swabia as anti-king, January—March 1077 126

CHAPTER XIII.

The struggle in Germany between Henry and Rudolf—Death of Rudolf—Wibert, archbishop of Ravenna, elected anti-pope—

CONTENTS xiii

Henry crowned by the anti-pope in Rome—Rome occupied by Robert Wiscard—Sack of Rome—Death of Gregory—Estimate of his character and work—Death of Robert Wiscard, 1077–85 137

CHAPTER XIV.

Pontificate of Victor III.—Election of Urban II.—Revolt of Henry's son Conrad—The Councils of Piacenza and Clermont —Proclamation of the first crusade—Reception of Urban II. at Rome, 1086–96 158

CHAPTER XV.

Close of the pontificate of Urban II.—Election of Pascal II.— Revolt of Henry, son of Henry IV.—Death of Henry IV.— His character, 1096–1106 170

CHAPTER XVI.

Character of Henry V. and of Pascal II.—Council of Troyes— Henry's visit to Italy—Scene in St. Peter's, Rome—Coronation of Henry V.—Strife between Henry and Pascal—Death of the pope, 1106–18 187

CHAPTER XVII.

Pontificate of Gelasius II.—Election of Calixtus II.—Conference at Strasburg—Council of Reims—Conference at Mouzon— Council of Worms—The Concordat and end of the investiture strife, 1118–23 203

INDEX 221

CHRONOLOGICAL TABLE OF SOME EVENTS REFERRED TO IN THIS VOLUME.

	A.D.
End of the separate Western Empire	476
Appeal of pope Gregory III. to Charles Martel	741
The Exarchate of Ravenna conquered by the Lombards	752
Pippin the Little anointed king of the Franks at Mainz	752
Charles the Great crowned emperor at Rome	800
Otto the Great crowned emperor at Rome	962
Birth of Hildebrand	(about) 1020
Normans begin to occupy Apulia	(about) 1040
Synod at Sutri and coronation of Henry III. at Rome	1046
Council of Reims	1049
Birth of Henry IV.	1050
Death of Henry III.	1056
Great Lateran Council	1059
Conquest of Sicily by the Normans	1061–4
Invasion of England by William the Conqueror	1066
Marriage of Henry IV.	1066
Hildebrand elected pope	1073
Revolt of the Saxons	1073
Synod at Rome forbidding lay investiture	1075
Council at Worms, Gregory VII. deposed	January 24, 1076
Synod at Rome, Henry IV. deposed	February 21, 1076
Diet of Tribur	October 16, 1076
Meeting of Henry IV. and Gregory VII. at Canossa,	January 28, 1077
Rudolf, duke of Swabia, elected anti-king	March 15, 1077
Wibert of Ravenna elected anti-pope	1080
Death of Rudolf of Swabia	1080
Sack of Rome by Robert Wiscard's troops	1084
Death of Gregory VII.	May 27, 1085
Death of Robert Wiscard	July 17, 1085
Council of Clermont (proclamation of the 1st Crusade)	November 18, 1095
Synod of Bari	1098
Death of Henry IV.	1106
Coronation of Henry V. at Rome	1111
Council of Reims	1119
Council of Worms, the Concordat	1122
Ratification of the Concordat at Rome, end of the investiture strife	1123

List of Popes and Contemporary Sovereigns.

POPES	GERMAN EMPERORS	KINGS OF FRANCE	KINGS OF ENGLAND
A.D.	A.D.	A.D.	A.D.
1033 Benedict IX. deposed . 1046	1039 Henry III. 1056	1033 Henry I. 1060	1035 Harold, son of Cnut 1040
1044 Sylvester III. deposed . 1046			1042 Harthacnut . 1042
1046 Gregory VI. deposed . 1046			1042 Eadward the Confessor . 1066
1046 Clement II. (Suidger) died 1047			
1048 Damasus II. (Poppo) died 1048			
1049 Leo IX. (Bruno) died . 1054			
1054 Victor II. (Gebhard) died 1057			
1057 Stephen IX. (Frederick) died . 1058	1056 Henry IV. 1106		
1058 Benedict X. deposed . 1059			
1059 Nicolas II. (Gerhard) died 1061		1060 Philip I. 1108	
1061 Alexander II. (Anselm of Lucca) died . 1073			1066 Harold . 1066
[1061 Honorius II. (Cadalus), anti-pope, died 1072]			1066 William I. 1087
1073 Gregory VII. (Hildebrand) died 1085			
[1080 Clement III. (Wibert), anti-pope, died 1100]			
1086 Victor III. (Desiderius) died 1087			1087 William II. . 1100
1088 Urban II. (Otto) died 1099			
1099 Pascal II. (Rainerius) died 1118	1106 Henry V. 1125		1100 Henry I. . 1135
[1118 Gregory VIII. (Burdinus), anti-pope, died 1121]	Anti-kings.		
1118 Gelasius II. (John of Gaeta) died 1119	1077 Rudolf of Swabia 1080	1108 Louis VI. 1137	
1119 Calixtus II. (Guido of Vienne) died . 1124	1081 Herman of Luxemburg 1090		

HILDEBRAND.

CHAPTER I.

INTRODUCTORY.

THE history of the Christian Church is a record of contests with the world. This antagonism, foretold by the

Church history a record of contests with the world

Divine Founder of the Church, we know must last as long as the world itself. But by the world, as opposed to the Church, we mean simply the most dominant form of evil at any given time; and therefore the character and complexion of the strife, and the nature of the questions upon which the issue is put, will vary according to the circumstances of every age.

During the first three centuries the struggle of the Church was mainly one for existence—first with Judaism or an insidious mixture of Judaism and Oriental philosophy; and, secondly, with the iron despotism of a pagan empire endeavouring to crush a religion which would admit no rival and recognised a higher law than the edicts of emperors.

After the conversion of Constantine in the fourth century the struggle was for the truth—for the preservation of the faith from manifold and subtle forms of error, for the protection of Christian morals from the baleful influence of heathen practices, ideas, and sentiments with which society in an age of decadent civilisation was deeply infected.

The third great contest was with the strong, rough races which from the end of the fourth century steadily forced their way into the old Roman empire, and gradually broke it up. Amidst the general wreck the Church stood the shock of invasion, and tamed and educated the conquerors. But the Church itself suffered severely in the effort. In the struggle for rights which was continually going on from the beginning of the fifth century, between the Church and the barbarian kings, the character of the clergy deteriorated; they became more secular and less learned. It is idle to conjecture how far this degradation of the Church would have gone, had it not been arrested by a singular train of events ending in the elevation of the Teutonic king, Charles the Great, to the throne of the Roman Empire in the West, and the firm establishment of the idea—to last for ages—that the Empire being co-extensive with the Church, must be ruled by two heads, the temporal and the spiritual—the emperor and the pope. By the foundation of a close alliance between these two central powers, Western Christendom was saved from grave disorder; but a conflict between them sooner or later was inevitable, and after the death of Charles the contest of the Church with the world came to mean a struggle for rights between these two forces, between royal and ecclesiastical authority, between the emperor or smaller sovereigns endeavouring to control the Church, and the Church asserting its claims to independence. The first acute stage in this contest was reached in the eleventh century. But to understand clearly the conditions of the strife, it is necessary to trace, however briefly, how the connexion between the Papacy and Teutonic kings north of the Alps grew up; although to do this we have to go back a long way.

In the middle of the eighth century the Papacy was in a feeble and perilous condition. The line of the Western emperors had long since come to an end (476). Italy was nominally subject to the emperors at Constantinople, but the exarchate of Ravenna where their vicegerents had ruled since the days of Justinian, was crumbling away beneath the pressure of the Lombards, who held all Italy in their hands except the extreme south, and some small bits of territory round Rome, Venice, and Naples. Although the Lombards had been settled in the country for nearly two hundred years, and had become Christians, they were still a rude, half-barbarous people, and an implacable hostility existed between them and the Papal See. Rome lay between the Lombard kingdom on the north, of which the capital was Pavia, and the great Lombard duchies of Benevento and Spoleto on the south. When the dukes were in rebellion (739), Rome had aided them, and the Lombard king Liutprand threatened to take vengeance on the city by annexing it to his dominions. Where could the pope, Gregory III., turn for help?

Origin of connexion between the Papacy and trans-Alpine sovereigns

The exarch (he was the last) was powerless. The emperor Leo the Isaurian was odious to the pope, and to the Italian Church from his attempts to enforce his edicts against the use of images in Christian worship. The pope looked beyond the Alps for the succour which was not to be found in the emperor or the exarch. Charles Martel the Frank, mayor of the palace in name, but king in power, had earned the gratitude of Christendom by his great victory over the Saracens at Tours A.D. 732. The deliverer of Gaul from the dreaded Saracen was implored to save Rome from the detested Lombard. The appeal, accompanied by an offer of the title of consul, was graciously received, and although it was so soon followed by the deaths of Charles and of the pope (741) that nothing directly came of it, yet none the less was it an event of extreme significance. It was a decisive break in the connexion between Rome and Constantinople; it prepared the way for the revival of the Western Empire in a new shape, it was the first step towards that alliance between the Papacy and a Teutonic power beyond the Alps which was to last for ages, and to shape both for good and evil the future destinies of Europe.

1. The pope and Charles Martel, A.D. 740

The next step in this remarkable alliance between the Papacy and the Franks is more startling. Pippin the Little, son of Charles Martel, resolved that the strange fiction should cease by which for more than fifty years the royal title had been held by the family of Clovis, while the royal power was wielded by the hereditary mayors of the palace. He willed that the name and the reality should at last be united

2. Pippin the Little, 752

in one person—himself. But it was not enough for him to be elected by the people and uplifted on the buckler with shouts and clash of arms. The sanction of the Church must be given, in the person of the supreme pontiff. The assent of pope Zacharias was asked and obtained: Childeric III., last of the Merovingian phantom kings, was quietly transferred from his palace to a cloister, and Pippin, having been proclaimed king at Soissons, was anointed at Mainz (752) by the saintly Boniface, the English apostle of Germany. Two years later pope Stephen II. visited the court of Pippin to crave for aid against the Lombards, and ratified the act of his predecessor by anointing Pippin and his two sons Charles and Carloman with his own hands at St. Denys. Pippin twice crossed the Alps, and twice defeated the Lombard king. The second time he wrested from the Lombards all the territory which they had taken from the emperor in North Italy, the Exarchate of Ravenna and the Flaminian Pentapolis, and bestowed it on the Holy See, receiving as his reward the title of Patrician. Thus, in return for a religious sanction, the Papacy received a material advantage, not only in the form of territory, but also of increased dignity in the eyes of the world. The pope had been appealed to as arbiter in the political crisis of a powerful people; at his word one king had been put down, another set up. It was only natural that the new dynasty should become the protector of the Papacy which had called it into existence. The real donation also of Pippin was soon followed by the appearance of what purported to be a far more ancient grant, the forged Donation of Constantine, and thus fact and fiction combined to swell the papal power, to lay the groundwork for vast pretensions, and all the mighty struggles which were to grow out of them.

But events still more momentous were to seal the alliance between the Papacy and the Franks. Twenty years after the death of Pippin his son Charles became by the death of his brother sole king. It had been a dark and troublous time in Rome; the election of the pope had been the occasion of ferocious and bloody tumults; a brief interval of peace with the Lombards had been succeeded by the old traditional hostility. In the pontificate of Hadrian I. (772-795) Rome was again threatened by the Lombard king, Desiderius; and once more a passionate cry for help was made to the king of the Franks. Charles crossed the Alps with a powerful force. Pavia was taken, after an obstinate resistance; Desiderius vanished into a monastery, the native line of Lombard kings came to an end, and northern Italy became a part of the Frankish dominions.

<small>3. Charles the Great</small>

The pope, the Roman clergy, the senate, the nobles, the people, hailed Charles as a deliverer. He was embraced by the pope on the steps of St. Peter's; he devoutly attended the ceremonies of Holy Week, and at the close he solemnly ratified the donation made by his father Pippin. Hadrian died in 795. His successor, Leo III., having been nearly murdered by a band of conspirators, fled to the court of Charles; but the accusations of his enemies followed him there, and Charles resolved to try his cause in Rome. This he did in December, 800; the charges were heard in open synod, the pope was acquitted, the conspirators sentenced. And then followed the memorable act which is a turning-point in the history of Europe.

At the close of the solemn service in St. Peter's on Christmas Day, the pope advanced to the king as he knelt before the high altar, and placed a crown upon his head, while the multitude broke forth into a shout, 'To Charles, the most pious Augustus, crowned by God, the great and pacific Emperor, be life and victory!' Charles, the king of the Franks, the conqueror of the Lombards, the Saxons, and the Avars, the protector of Christendom against the Saracens and the Northmen, rose from his knees, on that wonderful day, bearing a title greater than all others— a title laden with mighty memories of the past, and charged with mighty consequences for the future.

Charles crowned emperor

Charles was worthy, by his genius and achievements, to receive that august title. It did not indeed confer any powers upon him which he had not exercised, or might not have exercised, as Patrician of Rome. But the possession of the title was in itself a power—the power inherent in a venerable name. Its splendour shed a lustre and dignity upon him who bore it, which was of incomparable value. And the rise of a man fitted to play the part of emperor in the West, coincided with the lapse of imperial power at Constantinople into degradation and contempt. Rome would not acknowledge Irene as empress, who had deposed and blinded her own son. In the eyes of the Romans the imperial throne was vacant; the worthiest man in Christendom had now been elected to fill it; he had been crowned in the old capital by the supreme pontiff, and Rome was once

Consequences of this event

more the seat of empire—an empire which was enlarged by the recovery of Gaul and the addition of Germany. Although the line of emperors went on at Constantinople until the capture of the city by the Turks in 1453, yet from the crowning of Charles I., 800, the only emperors acknowledged by Western Europe were those who were crowned at Rome, or at least by the Roman pontiff. The Roman Empire was thus revived in the West by the coronation of Charles, but in a new shape. It was henceforth to be 'the Roman Empire of the German nation;' the temporal head was to be (with some rare and insignificant exceptions) the German king elected by the German people; the spiritual head was the pope, who bestowed the imperial crown upon the elected king, who was not, strictly speaking, emperor until he had received it.

It is easy to see how future contests between these two powers were inevitable. The coronation of Charles was not performed by virtue of any ancient precedent or legal right; it was a unique act, justified by the circumstances of the moment and the unanimity of those who were concerned in effecting it. It started the idea, which became firmly fixed, that the German king should be Roman emperor, and that he must be crowned by the pope; but the precise relations between these two potentates were nowhere defined. If the pope bestowed the crown, had he the power to withhold it, or was he bound to yield to the choice of the people? If he was thus bound, and yet refused to ratify it, could the emperor-elect set up another pope in his place, and receive coronation at his hands. Again, was the

[margin: Contests inevitable after the death of Charles]

INTRODUCTORY

assent of the emperor a necessary condition of validity in the election of a pope? How far might the spiritual head of the empire command the subjects of the temporal head, or even the emperor himself? If he outrageously exceeded the bounds of his authority, could the emperor deal with him like a rebel? or if he grossly failed in the duties of his high office, could he be deposed from it? And so, on the other hand, if the emperor failed to do his duty as the protector of the Church and the guardian of the Christian faith and Christian morals, could the pope remove the crown which he had placed on an unworthy head? Nearly all these questions had to be dealt with; some of them were fought out during the epoch with which this volume is concerned.

But as long as Charles the Great lived they could not arise. Of the two powers which swayed Christen-

but could not arise in his lifetime

dom he was indisputably the greater. The will of Charles was everywhere supreme. The councils in which he presided were ecclesiastical synods no less than national diets; the compilation of public acts called 'Capitularies' contains laws and regulations concerning the conduct of the clergy, the discipline, the practice, and even the belief of the Church, as well as all manner of secular affairs. The great prelates were practically appointed by him, and were subject to the visitation of his officials. Even the pope, although in a spiritual sense his father and guide, had, in the technical phase of the day, 'adored' him at his coronation—that is to say, had prostrated himself at his feet, and so in some sense seemed to have become his subject.

As long, then, as Charles lived, the impress of one mind was felt everywhere; but when his master-mind was removed the dissolution of his vast empire was inevitable, even if it had not been partitioned amongst his sons. The change did not, indeed, come suddenly; there were sixteen years of stable government under Louis the Pious, but with the rebellion of his sons, about 830, the break-up began. The Frankish dominions were divided amongst them, and the remainder of the century was filled with strife between them and their descendants. The imperial crown was shifted from one branch of the family to another. Internally the Empire was distracted by incessant struggles between rival powers— kings, dukes, counts, bishops, abbots; outwardly it was threatened by barbarian invaders, the Magyars and the Northmen. Everywhere there was a tendency to disruption, and nowhere more than in Italy. It was divided into many lordships, often at war with one another. Rome was ruled sometimes by the pope, sometimes by the people, more often by some fierce nobles of the neighbourhood, who were called, or called themselves, consuls and patricians. The crown of Lombardy was the prize for which pretenders fought.

Break-up of the Empire in the 9th century

The only bond of union amongst all the jarring elements of this turbulent time was the Church. Whilst the Empire was divided, the Church was still one. But the Church itself was deeply tainted with the general corruption. The worldly wealth and influence of the clergy increased, but it was at the expense of learning, culture, and sanctity of life. The spiritual life of the Church was becoming strangled in

Corruption of the Church

the bands of feudalism. Prelates were great feudal beneficiaries. In defiance of the laws of Charles, the bishops rode to war; rich bishoprics and abbeys became objects of ambition to greedy competitors, and king or emperor was tempted to bestow them, for service or for money, upon unworthy candidates. The clergy were commonly married, and there was a tendency amongst the ecclesiastical aristocracy to become an hereditary caste, transmitting their benefices to members of their own rank and resenting the elevation of men of humbler birth. Had this gone on the clergy would have become intensely local in their sympathies; the divisions of the Church would have followed the divisions of the Empire, and its dependence on the Papacy, as the central and supreme authority, would have been loosened. During the latter part of the ninth century and the whole of the tenth, the three evils were steadily growing with which Hildebrand afterwards waged implacable war—clerical marriage, simony, and investiture by lay hands.

Nor did the Papacy itself escape the general corruption. The highest point to which papal claims had ever been carried was reached in the pontificate of Nicolas I. (858–867), whose pretensions were aided by the famous forgery, now first made public, known as the Decretals of Isidore. In the imperious tone of his judgment between rival candidates for the see of Constantinople, in his stern prohibition of the divorce of king Lothair from his queen, in his bold assumption of authority over the prelates of Germany and Gaul, Nicolas is a kind of anticipation of Hildebrand. But this gleam of grandeur and power was followed by a century of the most profound darkness. The papal throne was won by every species of violence and intrigue. For fifty years it was at the disposal of three profligate women, in league with licentious nobles and foreign adventurers.

From this abyss of infamy and shame the Papacy was rescued for a time by the Saxon emperor Otto the Great. The direct line of Charles the Great in Germany had come to an end in 911 A.D. First Conrad of Franconia, and then his rival, Henry of Saxony, were elected to the throne. Otto I., the son of Henry, was by far the ablest king who had risen in Germany since Charles, and in some sort revived the work which had been so largely undone after his death. He suppressed rebellion and disorder in his kingdom; he vanquished the savage Magyars on the eastern border in the bloody battle of the Lechfeld; he subdued the remnants of Lombard power in Northern Italy. At the invitation of pope John XII., he visited Rome (962) to free the city from the tyranny of the nobles, and the imperial crown was bestowed upon him there, as the title had already been given him by his victorious host after the battle of the Lechfeld (955). The tie between Rome and Germany, begun by Pippin and Charles, was made fast by Otto; the possibility of an independent Italian state was indefinitely postponed, and the 'Roman Empire of the German nation' was definitely established.

Otto the Great ruled as vigorously in Italy as elsewhere. He subdued the turbulent lords of the Romagna, he deposed pope John XII., set up Leo VIII. in his stead, and made the Romans swear not to elect any pontiff in future whom he had not approved. Otto's grandson, Otto III., followed in his footsteps with yet more ambitious aims. He placed Germans in the papal chair, for in truth Christendom could no longer tolerate the ignorant and licentious Italians who had disgraced the Holy See. His kinsman and chaplain, Bruno (Gregory V.), a man of austere morals, was his first nominee, and was succeeded by Sylvester II., the pious, eloquent, and learned Gerbert. Otto was fascinated by the magic influence of Rome, and purposed making the ancient capital once more the residence of the emperor. But this and all his other projects, many of them great and wonderful, were cut short by premature death at the age of twenty-two, and the direct line of the Ottos came to an end in 1002 A.D. The successors of Otto, Henry II. (1002-1024) and Conrad II. (1024-1034), were for the most part too much occupied with repressing disorder in Germany to bestow much attention upon Rome. Henry II., indeed, had noble schemes of Church reform, but they were frustrated by his death; and for the first forty years of the eleventh century the popes were the nominees—generally the simoniacal nominees—of the counts of Tusculum, and the Church sank into a condition of deeper corruption in Italy than in any part of Christendom. In Gaul and Germany, however, a spirit of religious reform, of which the great monastic house of Clugny in Burgundy was the chief source and centre, was beginning to work upon public opinion, and Henry III., the son of Conrad, became thoroughly animated by this spirit. Under his influence, and that of the German popes whom he appointed, the reformation of the Church began, which was to be carried on and consummated by Hildebrand and his successors. Under Henry III. there was the most complete concord which ever existed between the spiritual and temporal heads of the Holy Roman Empire. Under his son Henry IV. began the first great struggle between them for supremacy.

CHAPTER II.

DEGRADATION OF THE PAPACY. BEGINNING OF A REFORMATION UNDER HENRY III. THE RISE OF HILDEBRAND. 1033-47.

THE degradation of the Papacy under the counts of Tusculum reached its lowest depth when a boy of twelve years of age, who took the title of Benedict IX., was seated in the papal chair. As he grew up to manhood Benedict led a life of shameful depravity, and the condition of Rome became deplorable; the people were relapsing into barbarism, the churches were falling to pieces, pilgrims to the holy places were mercilessly plundered, and returned home declaring that the sacred city was a den of robbers and murderers of whom the pope and his minions were the chief captains. At the end of ten years the patience of the Romans was exhausted. Benedict was deposed and driven from the city, and John, bishop of Sabina, elected in his place, under the name of Sylvester III., but through the intrigues of the Tusculan faction he was soon expelled and Benedict reinstated. Benedict, however, from weariness of the office—possibly, as some

Degradation of the Papacy, 1033

DEGRADATION OF THE PAPACY

chroniclers say, from a desire to marry his cousin—or from simple greed, sold the Papacy to the archpresbyter, John Gratian, who assumed the name of Gregory VI. Gregory belonged to a party of reformers in Rome who were disciples of the school of Clugny; he was a man of some learning and of chaste life, but he had accumulated great wealth, and seems to have persuaded himself that a part of it might be piously expended in the purchase of the papal throne. At any rate when he had become pope he was conscientious in his administration. He did his best to repair the churches, to put down plunder, and to recover the property of the see which had been lost through violence or fraud. The Tusculan nobles, however, were not yet baffled, and succeeded in bringing back their wretched nominee once more against his will. There were now three claimants for the Papacy, each in arms against the others, each occupying a portion of the city; Benedict held the Lateran, Gregory Sta. Maria Maggiore, Sylvester St. Peter's. The scandal and confusion of the situation were now intolerable. Peter, archdeacon of Rome, called a large meeting of bishops, clergy, monks, and laity, at which it was resolved to invoke the aid of the German king. Peter hastened over the Alps to the court of Henry, and, kneeling before him, besought him with tears to rescue Rome from misery and shame. Henry responded to the appeal; he was a religious, upright sovereign, who had long striven to check simony and other corruptions of the Church in his own dominions; and it would have ill become such a king to receive the imperial crown from a simoniacal

Three claimants for the Papacy

Appeal to the king, Henry III. 1046

pope. He crossed the Alps in the autumn, and was received with great honour at Pavia (October 25) by Boniface, marquis of Tuscany, and other nobles. At Piacenza pope Gregory appeared and was treated with the respect due to his office; the king reserving his judgment upon the three rivals for a great synod which he proposed to hold at Sutri about thirty miles north of Rome.

The synod met on December 20. The king was present, but Gregory was permitted to preside. The claim of Sylvester was soon settled; he was convicted of simony, deposed from the Papacy, degraded from the priesthood, and condemned to retire into a monastery. As for Gregory, he frankly confessed his purchase of the papal throne from Benedict; his only defence was that he had been actuated by a sincere desire for the welfare of the Church, but his conscience now smote him; he pronounced himself guilty of simony and unworthy of his high office; he tore off his pontifical robes, and descended from his chair, and his self-condemnation was formally ratified by the council.

Synod at Sutri, 1046

The king now proceeded to Rome and entered it without any opposition. Another large synod was held in St. Peter's on December 23 and 24, and Benedict, who had not appeared at Sutri, was solemnly deposed. The work of reformation had been vigorously begun, in the right way and in the right place. The capital of Christendom was purged from unworthy pretenders to the papal chair, which was now vacant for the fittest man who might be found to fill it. But where was he to be found? So degenerate were the Italian clergy that few or none could be sug-

Henry nominates a new pope, Clement II.

gested who were not disqualified, either by lack of learning or by simony, or vices of a darker kind. The king therefore was asked to nominate whom he would. He first named Adalbert, archbishop of Bremen, a man of ability, learning, and high birth, of whom we shall presently hear much more. But Adalbert declined the perilous dignity, and the king's choice then fell upon Suidger, bishop of Bamberg, a prelate of unblemished life and unquestioned piety. His reluctance to leave his native land and his bishopric was overborne by the entreaties of the king, the people, and the clergy. It was objected, indeed, by some that no one who had not been ordained in the Church of Rome could canonically be elected pope, but the canons laid down the principle that times of urgent need justified exceptions to the rule, and Henry took his stand on this ground. He himself led the bishop to the papal chair, the people expressed their assent by acclamation, and the name of Clement II. which Suidger now assumed, having been borne by the immediate successor of St. Peter, was deemed a happy augury of a new line of apostolic popes.

On Christmas day, in St. Peter's church, Henry, with his wife, Agnes of Poictiers, received the imperial crown at the hands of the new pope. On the same festival, and in the same place, nearly two hundred and fifty years before, the crown had been bestowed upon Charles the Great, and now when the temporal and spiritual heads of the Empire were once more men worthy of their high and sacred dignities, the prospect of a bright future seemed to dawn on Christendom. It was a proud day for the German nation when a German king received the imperial crown, in the capital of the Western world, from a German pope nominated by himself. Nothing could exceed the deference paid to the emperor by the Romans. To strengthen his authority in the city, the title of Patrician, which had been usurped by the tyrannising nobles, was added to that of Emperor, and the oath which Otto the Great had wrung from the people by force was now spontaneously taken, that no one should be elected pope without the approbation of the emperor.

Clement promptly set about his task of reformation. He held a synod in January (1047), at which severe
Reformation under Clement II. decrees were passed against simony. Men convicted of buying or selling sacred offices were to be punished with excommunication; clerics who had been ordained by bishops whom they knew to be simoniacal, were to be subjected to penance and suspension for forty days. A strife for precedence between the bishops of Ravenna, Aquileia, and Milan, was settled in favour of the See of Ravenna, which had lately been given to a German, Humphrey, the Imperial Chancellor for Italy.

Whilst the Pope was redressing the disorders of the Church, the emperor was reducing the strongholds
The Normans in Southern Italy of turbulent nobles in the neighbourhood of Rome, after which pope and emperor went together into Southern Italy to assert their authority over the Lombard and Norman nobles. Thirty years only had elapsed since a small band of Normans, on their return from a pilgrimage to Palestine, had saved Salerno from destruction by a Saracen fleet

(1016). From that time the stream of Norman adventurers had never ceased to flow into the southern parts of Italy. Norman knights commanded by William Iron-arm, son of Tancred of Hauteville, won a splendid victory over the Saracens in Sicily in 1039, leading the van of the Greek army under the standard of George Maniakês. But their services were ill requited, and they then resolved to reward themselves with the conquest of Apulia. Army after army commanded by the catapans, as the vice-gerents of the Eastern emperors were called, was vanquished by the hardy warriors of the North; Normans and Lombards, sometimes in alliance, sometimes at war with each other, were continually pressing southwards and wresting the country, piece by piece, from the Eastern Empire. It was of the highest importance for the stability of the Western Empire and of the Papacy that these powerful people should not establish an independent kingdom. Waimar, the Lombard prince of Salerno, had already invested Drogo, a brother of William Iron-arm, and Radulf, another Norman, with the lordships of Apulia and Calabria. Henry now compelled Waimar to renounce his claim to suzerainty; Drogo and Radulf were re-invested by the emperor himself, and together with Waimar did homage to him as their over-lord. The spiritual supremacy of the pope followed as a matter of course. The pallium was bestowed on the archbishop of Salerno, and his metropolitan privileges were confirmed. The importance of these events can hardly be overrated. The conquest of Apulia by the Normans was a direct aggression of Western power upon the possessions of the Eastern Empire; the visit of Henry and the pope definitely bound the conquerors and their conquests to the Roman Empire of the German nation.

Early in the spring Henry moved northwards. The Lombard princes of Benevento, Pandulf and Landulf, remained faithful to the Eastern Emperor, and closed their gates against Henry. They were excommunicated by the pope, and the city was left to suffer a severe chastisement at the hands of the emperor's Norman vassals. He himself travelled up the eastern coast, spent Easter at Ravenna, visited Mantua and Verona, crossed the Brenner in May, and reached Speier in time for Whitsuntide.

Return of the emperor to Germany, 1047

The deposed pope Gregory was compelled to follow the emperor into Germany, and he was accompanied by his chaplain, a young man of small stature and ungainly figure, feeble in voice, dull of complexion, but with a bright piercing eye, bespeaking a fiery spirit, and a mind of restless activity and uncommon penetration. This was Hildebrand. He was now about twenty-six years of age, and the few facts which can be picked out of the mass of legends with which the malice of enemies, or the veneration of friends, have overlaid the real history of his early life, may be summed up in a few words. He was born in the hamlet of Rovaco near Soana, a small town in the Tuscan marshes, a few miles from Orbitello. Soana is now a poor, ruinous, fever-stricken village, and the cathedral, a building of the eleventh century, is the only vestige of its former prosperity, and the only direct link with the days of Hildebrand. His father's name was Bonizo; his mother's is unknown. His own name points to some Teutonic connexion of the family; and being

Early life of Hildebrand

DEGRADATION OF THE PAPACY

supposed by contemporaries to signify Hell-brand or 'pure flame,' it probably suggested many of the later stories about fire being seen to issue from his head or raiment; but by enemies, and Protestants (including the writer of one of our Homilies), it was understood in the opprobrious sense of 'firebrand.' That his father was a carpenter or, as some chroniclers say, a goatherd, there is no trustworthy evidence: still less that he belonged to the noble family of the Aldobrandini, a connexion no doubt suggested by the name given to the son. Hildebrand's parents, however, had relations in Rome who held high positions. His maternal uncle was the abbot of St. Mary's on the Aventine, and as such held the third place among the twenty abbots who assisted the pope when he celebrated mass.

From notices in Hildebrand's letters it may be inferred that he was educated here with other boys, many of them of high birth.[1] Here also he probably first acquired that peculiar veneration for the Blessed Virgin which he retained through life. The house of St. Mary was the abode of the abbot of Clugny when he visited Rome; it was the retreat of Laurentius, the learned bishop of Amalfi; it was the centre of a group of earnest men, animated by the reforming spirit which marked all the disciples of the school of Clugny. According to one of the many legends of Hildebrand's boyhood, it was Odilo, the abbot of Clugny, who saw sparks of fire issuing from his raiment, and predicted that, like John the Baptist, he would be 'great in the sight of the Lord.' Such tales testify at least to the high estimate of his ability early formed by those who

[1] Epistles, i. 1; i. 39; iii. 21; vii. 23.

had good opportunities of observing him. He had made his profession as a monk, but was still only a youth when John Gratian, archpresbyter of the church of S. Giovanni by the Latin gate, took him into his service, probably as a subdeacon. He was about twenty-five years old when his patron became pope and made him his chaplain. It is singular that the most implacable opponent of simony should have begun his public career in the service of a man who had bought the papal chair. We can only suppose that in the view of Hildebrand, as of his patron, the act was justified as a means of rescuing the Papacy from the depths of infamy into which it had fallen. However obtained, it was better that the throne should be occupied by a good man than by a wild profligate. And as Hildebrand had not been ashamed to serve a patron who had risen by irregular means, it must be reckoned to his credit that he did not desert him in his fall. Gregory and his chaplain were entrusted by the emperor to the care of Herman, archbishop of Cöln, and in Cöln the deposed pope died in the following year, 1048. Hildebrand then went to Clugny (which according to some chroniclers he had already visited in early youth), and here he resided for a year. According to his own account he was enamoured of cloister life, and would gladly have embraced it for the rest of his days. He never ceased indeed to be a monk in austerity of life and rigour of discipline, but we may well doubt whether his fiery spirit and commanding genius would have acquiesced in perpetual seclusion. In Clugny we must now leave him for a time, to trace the course of events in Germany and Italy.

CHAPTER III.

PROGRESS OF THE REFORMING MOVEMENT. THE PONTIFICATE OF LEO IX. 1047-54.

WHILST the emperor had been asserting his authority in Italy, rebellion had broken out behind him, north of the Alps, amongst the nobles, who had resented his strong rule. Godfrey, duke of Lotharingia, was the leader of the insurgents, and before the emperor could attack them, Godfrey had taken Nimeguen and Verdun, and laid siege to Lüttich (Liège), where he was kept in check by the bishop.

Rebellion in Germany

The insurrection happening just when Henry seemed to have reached the height of his power was a blow to his happiness and hopes, and a very real cause of anxiety and alarm. It was impossible to forecast how far the spirit of revolt might spread. Boniface, marquis of Tuscany, the most powerful noble in Italy, was found to be in league with the malcontents in Germany—an alliance which instantly gave a shock to the settlement which Henry had made with the Lombards and Normans. Just at this critical moment pope Clement died. Envoys were despatched from Rome to the emperor, begging him to appoint a successor; but the Tusculan faction took advantage of the interval to reassert their power, and actually replaced their creature, Benedict, in the papal chair. Henry nominated Poppo, bishop of Brixen, a native of Bavaria, who had accompanied him to Italy, and Boniface of Tuscany was

Death of pope Clement II., October 9, 1047

directed to conduct the new pope to Rome (January 25, 1048); but the sympathies of Boniface were with the Tusculan counts as well as the German insurgents, and he refused to obey the order. Henry saw there was imminent risk of a network of rebellion spreading all round him. By a series of prompt and skilful movements he divided the confederates and thwarted their plans. Boniface no longer dared to disobey; he procured the removal of Benedict, and conducted the pope-elect to Rome, where he was consecrated in St. Peter's on July 17, under the name of Damasus II.

<small>Pope Damasus II. appointed</small>

In less than a month, however, the summer heat in Rome had proved fatal to the German pope, as it was destined to be to so many thousands of his countrymen. There were rumours that he and his predecessor had been poisoned, and it is not surprising that such sinister tales, however ill-founded, in addition to the natural difficulties and perils of the situation, increased the reluctance of northern prelates to accept the Papacy. Once more, however, the emperor was asked to fill the vacancy. A strong man in every sense of the word was needed for the office, and happily such a man was not wanting at this moment.

<small>Dies August 1048</small>

Bruno, bishop of Toul, was the model of a mediæval prelate: at once scholar, soldier, politician, and saint, he was fitted to play the part, according to circumstances, of general or statesman, abbot, bishop, or pope. He was a kinsman of the emperor, and had been well educated at the cathedral school of Toul, but early in his youth resided chiefly at the court of the emperor Conrad, where his

<small>Early life of Leo IX.</small>

goodness, and cleverness, combined with a handsome face and stately figure, made him a general favourite. In 1025, at the age of twenty-three, he was ordained deacon by the bishop of Toul, and soon afterwards was sent in command of the troops furnished by the bishop for the emperor Conrad's expedition to put down a rebellion at Milan. His military talents excited the admiration of the emperor and of the whole army. Whilst he was in Lombardy, Herman, bishop of Toul, died; the clergy and people unanimously elected Bruno, and sent an urgent request to the emperor to confirm their choice. Conrad had destined him for high preferment, and was unwilling to send him to a poor and distant bishopric, exposed to some perils, on the frontier of his kingdom. But Bruno thought that in the poverty of the see and the freedom of the election he saw a divine call to accept the office, and having obtained the emperor's consent, he took his departure, crossed the Alps (after narrowly escaping capture by the enemy), and arrived at Toul on Ascension Day 1027.

His diocese soon felt the vigour of his administration; simony was checked, and the monasteries rigorously reformed on the pattern of Clugny. He did good service also to the Empire by negotiating a peace between Conrad and Henry I., king of France, in 1032 ; a task for which he was well fitted by his familiarity with the tongues of Germany and Gaul, as well as by his uprightness and practical wisdom, which secured him general respect. He stood firmly by Henry III. in his contest with duke Godfrey, and it was probably through his influence that most of the Lotharingian prelates remained faithful to the emperor. He also paid a visit to the king of France, and arranged terms of peace between him and Henry, which deprived Godfrey of his hopes of support from French arms.

Such was the man whom the emperor now selected to fill the papal chair. The nomination took place at Worms, where Henry was keeping Christmas (1048). After three days spent in fasting and prayer Bruno yielded a reluctant consent; but he stipulated that the appointment should be ratified by the free choice of the Roman clergy and people. Until this should have been obtained he refused to assume any pontifical state. On his way through Burgundy he visited Clugny, and probably at the suggestion or command of Hugh the Prior, Hildebrand was appointed to accompany him to Rome. Hildebrand tells us [1] that, unwilling as he had been to leave Italy, he was now more unwilling to return. But his heart was soon won by the demeanour of Bruno, who travelled in the guise of a humble pilgrim; and the journey was not devoid of the marvellous incidents which, according to Bruno's biographer, attested his sanctity wherever he went. Celestial music was heard, and the swollen waters of the Teverone subsided to let the travellers pass over. As they drew near Rome they were met by a great concourse of people and clergy; Bruno entered the city barefoot, and professed himself ready to return if his appointment was not agreeable to them. Loud acclamations left no doubt of their approval, and on February 12, 1049, he was consecrated pope, under the name of Leo IX.

Accompanied by Hildebrand to Rome

Consecrated pope

[1] Epist. vii. 14A.

The short pontificates of his two predecessors, and the long vacancies between them, had brought the affairs of the Papacy into a state of sad confusion. But Leo was equal to the task of evolving order out of chaos, and he was seconded by a minister as courageous and astute as himself. The active career of Hildebrand begins from this point. Leo made him a cardinal subdeacon, and entrusted to him the chief supervision of finance. The exchequer was almost empty, but some timely offerings from the rich nobles of Benevento relieved immediate needs, and further funds were raised through the dealings of Hildebrand with Benedict, a rich converted Jew. By making friends with the popular leaders in the Trasteverine quarter, by careful husbanding of his resources, and judicious gifts, added to the weight of his personal influence, Hildebrand won the whole city over to the pope; even the Tusculan faction dissembled their chagrin and affected acquiescence. By Leo he was also appointed abbot of St. Paul's, where he introduced rigorous reforms, not before they were needed, if the tales be true that women waited on the monks in the refectory, and cattle were stabled in the church.

Leo was, in a literal sense, the most active pontiff who had ever occupied the papal chair; for he made his power felt in all parts of Christendom by personal visits, when possible, rather than by legates and letters. And in some sense he became all things to all men; in monasteries he appeared as the devout pilgrim, or preached to congregations of poor folk in the garb of a humble monk, or cast himself as a penitent prostrate before some sacred

His vigorous administration

shrine; but in making a journey to consecrate a church, or translate the relics of a saint, he rode in state on horseback, surrounded by a brilliant retinue of clergy and nobles. Miracles were supposed to be wrought by him wherever he went; over birds and beasts he exercised a magic power; a parrot presented to him by the king of Denmark was said to have uttered his name as soon as it saw him, without previous training; and a cock at Benevento displayed the same singular discernment. The fame of his wonder-working powers, joined to his genuine piety and goodness, increased the reverence with which men beheld him when he presided in full pontifical state at the great synods in which decrees were passed for the reformation of the Church.

In his first synod, held in Rome at Easter, and another held at Whitsuntide in Pavia, an attempt was made to put down simony and the marriage of the clergy by a decree that, all clergy implicated in simoniacal transactions, even if they had merely been ordained by bishops simoniacally appointed, should be degraded from their order. But it was found that such a remedy was too drastic for the times, as it would have involved the deprivation of more than half the clergy of Italy, and a consequent suspension of all religious offices. Leo, therefore, fell back upon a milder measure; after making a full confession, and submitting to penance, offenders might resume their functions. Decrees were also passed prohibiting marriage of the clergy, but now and for many years to come such decrees were practically futile.

Synod in Rome, Easter 1049

From Pavia Leo went to Germany. He joined the emperor in Saxony, and with him entered Cöln in great

state, when he invested the archbishop with the office of Archchancellor of the Apostolic See; and excommuni-
<small>Leo visits Germany</small> cated the rebellious Godfrey of Lotharingia, who was humbled to the dust by the blow. The duke prostrated himself before the emperor and pope at Aachen and obtained a pardon, but not the restoration of his duchy. He then went to Verdun and received a scourging before the altar of the ruined church, which he not only undertook to repair, but laboured in the work with his own hands.

Leo purposed to make his authority felt in Gaul no less than in Germany, and the clergy were summoned
<small>and France</small> to a great council to be held at Reims, on October 1, the festival of St. Remigius, when the pope proposed to translate the relics of the saint and consecrate the abbey church. More than a hundred years had passed since a pope had entered French territory, and in the interval the pretensions of the Papacy to œcumenical power had vastly increased. The prospect of the Gallican Church being subjected to a German pope, the nominee and intimate friend of the German emperor, was viewed with jealousy and alarm by the king, Henry I. He refused to attend the council, and he tried to hinder the attendance of the higher clergy by calling out his military array for an expedition against some rebel vassals; but the pope was firm, the clergy shrank from disobeying his citation, and the king made the best of what he could not help, by formally excusing some of the prelates from attendance on his expedition.

On October 1, therefore, the abbey church of St. Remigius was hallowed with great pomp; both the church and the great atrium in front were thronged with people, to whom the pope preached from a balcony; the relics of the saint were carried to the cathedral church, round the town and back to the abbey, followed by tumultuous crowds.

On October 3 the pope opened the council. He sat between four archbishops: of Lyons (the Primate of all Gaul), Trier (on which he had himself conferred metropolitan rights), Reims, and Besançon. Sixteen other bishops were present, and a large number of abbots. England was represented by Duduc, bishop of Wells (himself a Lotharingian), Wulfric, abbot of St. Augustine's, Canterbury, and Ælfwine, abbot of Ramsey.

<small>Council of Reims, 1049</small>

One of the first acts of the council was to declare that the pope alone had the right to be called the Apostolic Primate of the Church Universal, and the archbishop of St. James of Compostella, who had arrogated the title of apostolic, was excommunicated. Twelve canons were passed for the better ordering of the Church. They forbade simony, and enjoined freedom of election by clergy and people to ecclesiastical offices; the clergy were forbidden to marry or bear arms, or take any fees for burials, baptism, the administration of the eucharist, or visitation of the sick. The practice of usury, the plunder of the poor and of pilgrims, and marriage within the prohibited degrees were all condemned.

Bishops and abbots accused of simony and other crimes were tried by the council. Two were deposed: Wido, archbishop of Reims, narrowly escaped deposition on a charge of simony, and his case was deferred for hearing at Rome. The archbishop of Sens, and the bishops of Amiens, Beauvais, and Lyons were excommunicated for failing to appear at the council; their sees declared vacant, and the clergy and people directed to make fresh election. In all these dealings with the French clergy the peremptory tone of Leo, and the total absence of any reference to the will and pleasure of the king, is most remarkable. He issues his commands as the absolute sovereign of the Catholic Church.

From Reims Leo travelled, through Verdun and Metz, to Mainz, where a synod was held on October 19. The canons of Reims against simony were renewed, but there is no record of prelates being deprived or excommunicated in Germany, as in Gaul. The next two months were occupied in visiting monasteries in Germany, and granting or confirming privileges to them. Christmas he spent at Verona. In the following Lent he made a pilgrimage to Monte Gargano. Easter was spent in Rome, where a large synod was held, attended by fifty-five bishops and thirty-two abbots. At this council the teaching of Berengar of Tours, who upheld a real, as opposed to a material, presence in the holy eucharist, was condemned. The current dogma of the Church had a powerful advocate at the council in Lanfranc of Pavia, abbot of Bec in Normandy. At this council also appeared Ealdred, bishop of Worcester, and Herman, bishop of Ramsbury, craving a dispensation from the pope for king Eadward from his vow of pilgrimage to the Holy Land, owing to the disturbed state of his kingdom. The dispensation was granted, on condition that Eadward repaired or rebuilt a monastery in honour of

Synod in Rome 1050. Berengar's teaching condemned

St. Peter. He fulfilled the condition by founding the renowned abbey of Westminster.

After the synod at Rome, the indefatigable Leo made a progress in Southern Italy, where he was respect-
Leo visits Apulia fully received by the Normans, and Waimar of Salerno. Here he held a synod at which the decrees against simony were adopted, and Humbert, a Lotharingian who was skilled in the Greek tongue, was appointed archbishop for the island of Sicily. Benevento, which still resisted the authority of the Western emperor and the pope, was again laid under the ban of the Church, and at last the punishment produced its effect. The inhabitants ere long expelled their hostile nobles, and surrendered their city to the pope.

In September another synod was held at Vercelli, where the case of Berengar was again debated. In
Synod at Vercelli. Berengar again condemned Gaul public opinion, even among the clergy, was much divided concerning the doctrine. The king himself vacillated. At the present time he had imprisoned Berengar, whose cause was pleaded at the synod by a canon of Tours; but he was no match for Lanfranc, who again appeared as the champion of the right faith; Berengar was excommunicated, and his doctrine condemned. Berengar, however, treated the excommunication with contempt; he had many distinguished friends in Gaul, and the name of John
Hildebrand goes as legate to France Scotus Erigena, from whom he derived his tenets, was held in great honour there. The controversy raged high. In 1054, Hildebrand was sent to France as papal legate to compose the strife. The theological views of Hildebrand were never

so clearly defined as his political aims. Personally he seems to have been kindly disposed towards Berengar, and not violently opposed to his doctrine; but he was prepared to uphold what the pope and the council had declared to be the right faith. It was during this journey to France that he was often heard to ejaculate, 'Invincible are the faith and the arms of Rome,' and to cite the verse from the Psalms, 'Blessed are they who keep His testimonies and seek Him with their whole heart.' Such utterances seem rather to imply an effort to brace up the mind to an unpleasant duty; but with characteristic boldness he summoned a council to meet in Tours—the very stronghold of the enemy. Nothing very decisive, however, was effected there. Hildebrand having accepted a rather ambiguous avowal of belief that the bread and wine after consecration were really the body and blood of Christ, advised Berengar to come to Rome, and promised to defend him. The sojourn of Hildebrand in Gaul was shortened by the tidings that the pope had been taken captive by the Normans in Apulia. How this came to pass has now to be related.

At the beginning of the year 1051, both the emperor and the pope seemed to have reached the highest point of prosperity. A son, long desired and prayed for, had been born to the emperor at Goslar in December. He was baptized in Cöln by archbishop Herman, and Hugh, now abbot of Clugny, was his godfather; the nobles swore fealty to him, as the heir of the kingdom and the Empire. The consolidation and expansion of the Empire and the Church were now going on steadily together, and the idea of a universal dominion,

Birth of Henry IV. 1050

complete on its spiritual and temporal side, seemed within measurable distance of accomplishment; but the fair prospect was soon overclouded; the closing years of the emperor and the pope were harassed by anxiety and disaster; and the child of many hopes and prayers was destined to a tragical career of sorrow, which has few parallels even in the mournful annals of kings.

In 1051, disturbances broke out, almost together, on the Lotharingian and Hungarian borders of the Empire, which Henry attempted to quell with very imperfect success. But the greatest blow to imperial and papal power was to come from the other side of the Alps. The ambition of Leo was not confined to a moral reformation of the Church; it included also the maintenance and extension of papal territory. After the people of Benevento surrendered their city to the pope, he entrusted the defence of it to the Normans under Drogo. A fierce and sanguinary strife having broken out between them and the inhabitants, Leo, who seems to have assumed that the Normans had provoked the tumult, resolved to expel them by force from the whole territory of Benevento, if not from all Italy. But he had great difficulty in raising an army. The emperor was too much occupied by troubles in Germany to help him; and the king of France and nobles of Burgundy turned a deaf ear to his appeal, although accompanied with rich offers and a promise of remission of sins. Waimar of Salerno also refused to aid him, and warned him against attempting so vast an enterprise. But the pope would not desist from his purpose. At last a motley army,

Quarrel of Leo with the Normans in Apulia

made up of poor material from various parts of Italy, but strengthened by 500 Germans, was got together. Argyros, the catapan at Bari, agreed to support the papal forces, which were mustered, about the middle of June, at Civitate, some twelve miles from Benevento, on the borders of Apulia. Drogo had been slain at Benevento, and the Norman army, consisting of about 3,000 knights, was commanded by two of his brothers, Humphrey and Robert Wiscard, and their brother-in-law, Richard of Aversa. In fighting power the Normans were immeasurably superior to the enemy, but they were much straitened for supplies, and hampered by the difficulties of their position between the forces of the pope and of the catapan. The leaders, therefore, tried to make terms with the pope, offering to hold their conquests as his vassals, and to pay a yearly tribute to Rome. But their offers were scornfully rejected, and both sides prepared for battle. The unwarlike Italians broke and fled at the first onset of the Normans; the Germans alone stubbornly held their ground and fought on against overwhelming odds until scarcely a man was left. The pope and his retinue, from the walls of Civitate, beheld the overthrow of his army. They might well tremble for their lives; but, to their amazement, their terrible conquerors were suddenly transformed into humble servants and suppliants of the pontiff. Humphrey cast himself at the feet of Leo, craved release for himself and people from excommunication, and promised, on that condition, to conduct him safely to Benevento. The ban was removed, and the pope and his company were escorted to Benevento with all outward marks of respect.

Defeat and capture of Leo by the Normans, 1053

Here Leo sojourned for about nine months in a kind of honourable captivity, occupying himself with penitential and devotional exercises, works of charity, and the study of Greek, in which he became so far proficient as to read the Holy Scriptures in the Septuagint version.

Nevertheless he still nourished designs against the Normans, and renewed his overtures to Argyros at Bari. But the interference of the pope with Apulian affairs, and his negotiations with the catapan, excited the jealousy of the patriarch of Constantinople, Michael Cerularius, and combined with theological disputes to sharpen the strife for precedence between the two sees, which was gradually widening the breach between the Eastern and Western branches of the Church. The patriarch, in a letter to the bishop of Trani, denounced the heresies of the Latins, especially the use of un-

Leo's negotiation with Constantinople

leavened bread in the Eucharist; a warm correspondence was carried on by chosen representatives of both sides on this subject, and on the question of precedence, each pontiff laying claim to the title of Universal Bishop. Presently, however, there was a change of tone, seemingly due to the mediation of Argyros, and courteous letters passed between the pope and the patriarch. Without abating any of his pretensions, Leo expressed a hope that a lasting reconciliation between the two great divisions of Christendom might be effected. Three envoys were despatched to Constantinople: Frederick of Lotharingia, (brother to duke Godfrey and chancellor of the pope) cardinal Humbert, and Peter, the exiled bishop of Amalfi. They took a letter from Leo to the emperor Constantine (Monomachus), in which he expressed the liveliest desire to see friendship established between the two emperors, and exhorted Constantine to join with Henry in expelling the sacrilegious Normans from the territory of St. Peter.

Misfortune had certainly not broken the spirit of the intrepid Leo, but incessant exertions and anxieties, perhaps also his austere asceticism, were telling upon his health. On February 12, 1054, the anniversary of his consecration as pope, he celebrated Mass for the last time; he longed to spend Easter in Rome, and, leaving Benevento on March 12, he was conveyed in a litter to Capua. After a halt there of twelve days, he was carried to Rome, accompanied by the abbot of Monte Cassino. It was revealed to him in a dream that his last moments were to be spent in the church of the apostle for whose honour he had so manfully laboured. He was therefore conveyed from the Palace of the Lateran to St. Peter's, where he prayed fervently and with many tears before the altar, after which he was taken to the adjoining palace. Here he received the Eucharist and extreme unction, and commended his soul to God in a prayer of humble resignation, which he uttered in his native German tongue. He died on the following day in the fifty-third year of his age, and was buried according to his own desire near to the grave of Gregory the Great. His tomb soon became the scene of miracles, and his name was enrolled in the Calendar of Saints.

His death, April 19, 1054

CHAPTER IV.

PONTIFICATES OF VICTOR II. AND STEPHEN IX.
1054—59.

THE death of Leo was a critical event for the Papacy and the Empire. Hildebrand hastened back from France to Rome. It would have been easy for him to have loosened the bond which had for nearly ten years closely tied Italy and the Papacy to the German emperor. The German popes had not been popular in Rome; the Normans were strong in the south; in the north Beatrice, widow of the marquis Boniface of Tuscany, had married duke Godfrey of Lotharingia, and thus the most formidable rebel in the Empire became one of the most powerful territorial lords south of the Alps. His brother Frederick was a distinguished leader of the reforming Clugniac party, and Hildebrand might easily have secured his election to the papal chair, or have ascended it himself. But he was too wise and wary to venture on such a course. The reformation of the Church thus far had been the joint work of emperor and pope; and the hearty support of the emperor was essential to its progress. Nor, indeed, without his protection was Rome yet safe from attempts of the Tusculan counts to regain their ancient sway.

Hildebrand therefore led a deputation, appointed by the clergy and people, to the German Court, and begged the emperor to name a new pope, adding a request that his choice might fall upon Gebhard, bishop of Eichstadt. Gebhard was in the prime of life, wealthy, able, and well

VICTOR II. AND STEPHEN IX.

versed in ecclesiastical and political affairs—warmly, but not obsequiously, devoted to the emperor. In Bavaria, indeed, he was such a valuable support to the throne that Henry was very reluctant to part with him, and Gebhard himself shrank from the dignity which had proved fatal to so many of his countrymen. At last, nearly a year after the death of Leo, at a council held in Regensberg in March (1055) emperor and bishop yielded, and on April 13 Gebhard was consecrated in St. Peter's, Rome, taking the title of Victor II.

Election of pope Victor II.

The emperor soon followed the pope to Italy. The chief object of his visit was to assert his suzerainty over the new possessions of duke Godfrey. For this purpose he spent some time in Ferrara, Mantua, Guastalla, and other towns, conciliating the inhabitants by hearing complaints, and granting exemptions from taxes and burdensome services. Godfrey had sent messengers to him, repudiating any disloyal intentions, and Beatrice maintained her right to marry any man whom she deemed fittest to be the guardian of her property and children. But Henry seems to have mistrusted them both. Godfrey shunned a meeting with him, and betook himself to Baldwin of Flanders, who was still in revolt, while Beatrice, with her son and two daughters, were detained in a kind of honourable captivity at the emperor's court. Here her son and elder daughter died, leaving the younger one, Matilda, now about eight years old, the sole heiress of her parent's vast possessions.

The emperor visits Italy

Meanwhile Godfrey's brother cardinal Frederick had returned from Constantinople after an unsuccessful mission. He and his colleagues had been laden, indeed, with presents by the emperor, but of these they were robbed on their journey, and from the patriarch they brought back nothing but excommunications. Frederick prudently retired to Monte Cassino, and thus the power and ambition of the Lotharingian brothers were held for a time in check.

In the autumn of 1055 the emperor was recalled to Germany by tidings of a conspiracy. This he soon stifled by prompt and vigorous action, and Christmas was spent quietly at Zürich, where he betrothed his son Henry to Bertha, daughter of the margrave Odo of Turin and Adelheid of Susa. Adelheid was a woman of great ability and large possessions, and nearly connected by a former marriage with the emperor's family, and by this alliance between their children Henry hoped to establish a counterpoise to the power of Beatrice in Northern Italy.

The emperor spent Easter at Goslar. In June he was reconciled with duke Godfrey at Trier, and permitted him to take back his wife and stepdaughter. In September he was joined by the pope at Goslar, and went with him to Bodfeld, a royal hunting-seat in the Harz forest. Whilst staying there the terrible tidings came that a Saxon host, sent against the Wends, had been almost destroyed by the enemy, and that the leaders had perished in the overthrow. The news of this disaster was such a shock to the emperor that it brought on a fatal attack of fever. Conscious that his end was near, he declared his forgiveness of all his enemies, and required the pope, bishops, and nobles who were present to renew their allegiance to the young

Henry, whom, with the empress, he commended to the pope's special care.

On October 5, 1056, the great emperor breathed his last. He was barely thirty-nine years old, but the harassing cares and toils of his life had probably worn out his constitution. He was buried on his birthday, October 28, beside his parents in the cathedral church of Speier, not yet completed, and young Henry, now six years old, was forthwith conducted to Aachen and crowned there by the pope.

Death of Henry III.

Under the strong and righteous rule of Henry III., the empire reached the meridian of its power, and had it been internally united, it might have defied the world. External enemies were conquered, but the spirit of intrigue and turbulence amongst the German nobles was only held in check by constant vigilance and coercion. The large hereditary fiefs intended to be a support to the crown, were a perpetual source of anxiety and peril. During the long minority of Henry IV. they naturally grew in power and independence, and after he came to the throne the task of controlling them, which had taxed his father's capacities to the utmost, proved too much for his strength, especially when rebellion sheltered itself under the sanction of the Church.

Although the empress was nominally regent, the pope and duke Godfrey were really the two greatest potentates in the empire. Godfrey and Baldwin of Flanders both swore allegiance to Henry in the presence of the pope, at Cöln, in December, but they obtained at the same time all which they had striven for. Godfrey was reinstated in

Power of the pope and Godfrey of Lotharingia

his duchy and the rich inheritance of his wife in Tuscany; Baldwin recovered all the fiefs of which he had been deprived in Flanders, and secured Hennegau for his son. After spending Christmas with the young king at Regensberg the pope returned to Italy. He kept Easter in Rome, and then travelled northwards to meet duke Godfrey. He who had been forced to fly from Italy as a suspected rebel, now returned as the chief representative, in company with the pope, of imperial authority, while his brother Frederick, who had entered Monte Cassino as a simple monk, had become abbot of that rich and powerful house, and cardinal-priest of St. Chrysogonus in Rome.

But the partnership of pope and duke in the government of Italy was soon to be dissolved by death. Once more the southern climate asserted its baleful influence; on July 28 pope Victor died of fever at Arezzo; he was even younger than the late emperor, and his premature death cut short a career of great activity and still greater promise. It deprived the empress of her ablest and most trustworthy counsellor. His place was speedily filled by the brother of duke Godfrey. The cardinal-abbot of Monte Cassino was in Rome when pope Victor died; and the clergy and people, without waiting for the return of Hildebrand from Arezzo, or communicating with the empress, offered him the Papacy, which he seems to have accepted with little or no reluctance. He was consecrated on August 3, in St. Peter's, and took the name of Stephen IX. As ambassador at Constantinople he had been a bold upholder of Roman orthodoxy and Papal supremacy in the face of the patriarch and the emperor; he was a monk

<small>Death of Victor II., 1057</small>

VICTOR II. AND STEPHEN IX. 43

and a rigid disciplinarian. The Italian, Peter Damiani, abbot of Monte Avellana, an intimate friend of Hildebrand's, a model of monkish austerity, and the fierce foe of clerical marriage, was made, sorely against his will, cardinal-bishop of Ostia. The pope issued a brief against simony, and entrusted the promulgation and enforcement of it in Germany to an uncompromising zealot, a Lotharingian, Humbert, the cardinal-bishop of Silva Candida, whom he made arch-chancellor of the Papacy, in the place of the archbishop of Cöln. Humbert was the author of a treatise upon simony, in which he denounces lay investiture as the chief source of the evil. That lay hands—above all, female hands—should bestow the ring and staff, the symbols of spiritual office, was in his view a degrading and infamous scandal. The whole tendency of his teaching was to depreciate the imperial power; all the emperors, in his judgment, except Henry III., had promoted simony rather than checked it; the Papacy and the Empire were as soul and body; it was for the soul to instruct, the body to execute its instructions.

Treatise of Humbert on simony

This treatise of Humbert's may be said to mark the point from which the relations between the Papacy and the Empire begin to be somewhat strained. Stephen, however, did not wish to hazard a rupture with the imperial court. Hildebrand was therefore sent, near the close of the year (1057), to Germany, and obtained a confirmation of the pope's election from the empress Agnes.

Like Leo IX., pope Stephen was bent upon ridding Italy of the Norman intruders. To assist his brother Godfrey in this pious work, he did not disdain to make overtures to the heretical court of Constantinople, and he seems to have intended to use some of the treasures of Monte Cassino for the same purpose. But Death of his schemes were cut short by death. He fell Stephen IX., 1058 ill at Monte Cassino, in December, and at Christmas seemed to be on the point of death. A partial recovery emboldened him to return to Rome in March, but he was a dying man. He set out for Florence to hold a synod there, and concert measures with his brother against the Normans; paid a visit on the way to Vallambrosa, and died there in the arms of the holy Gualberto, the founder of the house.

The German popes had not been always popular in Germany, because they became too Italian. In Italy they were unpopular, partly because they were German, and put Germans into many of the best benefices; partly on account of the rigour with which they pressed unwelcome reforms upon the clergy. As long, however, as the popes were the nominees of the emperor, and backed by the force of his authority, resistance was out of the question.

But now the administration was in the hands of a weak woman. Hildebrand was still in Germany; and Irregular although the dying pope had forbidden the election of Benedict X. people, under pain of anathema, to appoint a successor before Hildebrand returned, the opportunity of making an independent election was too tempting to be resisted. The counts Gregory of Tusculum and Girard of Galeria, with the sons of Crescentius of Monticelli, and their partisans, having secured the city and the papal palaces with troops, placed John Mincius, bishop of Velletri, a Roman belonging to the family of Crescentius, on the papal throne, and compelled a priest of Ostia to consecrate him by night (April 5), with the title of Benedict X. Peter Damiani and the other cardinal-bishops pronounced ineffectual anathemas on the doers of this daring deed, and then dispersed, some to Monte Avellana, some to Florence, others to Monte Cassino.

At this critical moment Hildebrand returned to Italy from Germany, and hearing what had happened in Rome he halted at Florence. He saw the gravity of the crisis. If the Papacy were not rescued from the hands of the nobles it would sink into the old slough of corruption, and the work of reform would be entirely wrecked. Duke Godfrey alone could supply enough material force to expel the usurping pope; and as Godfrey himself was an advocate of reform, and the action of the Romans was a defiance of his authority rather than that of the empress, Hildebrand easily persuaded him to support the man whom he recommended for the papal chair. This was Gerhard, bishop of Florence, a Burgundian by birth, well known at the court of Henry III., who had bestowed the bishopric upon him. He was a strong reformer, of vigorous intellect, competent learning, and irreproachable morals. About Whitsuntide (1058), envoys were despatched to the imperial court at Augsburg, who obtained the ready assent of the empress to Gerhard's appointment. Near the end of the year duke Godfrey had raised the men and Hildebrand had raised the money deemed sufficient to ensure success. The scattered cardinals and their clergy re-assembled at Siena and elected Gerhard there on December 28. He immediately summoned a synod at Sutri, where Benedict was pronounced deposed and excommunicate; and then advanced with his supporters to Rome, where the soldiers of Godfrey, and the money of Hildebrand, soon secured the acquiescence of the people. Benedict fled first to Passerano, and then to Galeria. Gerhard was consecrated in St. Peter's on or about January 25, and took the name of Nicolas II.

<small>Nicolas II. pope, 1059</small>

For ten years Hildebrand had looked to the German emperor as the mainstay of the reforming movement in the Church, but a new idea seems henceforth to have taken hold of his mind. The weakness of the regency in Germany, which his recent visit to the court must have revealed to him, the unpopularity of German popes and prelates in Italy, especially in Lombardy, the strength of duke Godfrey in the northern half, and of the Normans in the southern half of the peninsula, led him to conceive the design of making the apostolic see the independent centre of all national life in Italy, the originating source and directing spirit of all religious movements, not only there but in every part of Western Christendom.

CHAPTER V.

PONTIFICATE OF NICOLAS II. ELECTION OF ALEXANDER II. AND OF THE ANTI-POPE CADALUS. 1059–62.

Two great foundations of papal power were laid in the pontificate of Nicolas II. One of these was an alliance with the Normans. The other was the decree passed immediately after his election at a great Lateran council that henceforth the election of the pope should be made by the cardinal-bishops, assisted by the other cardinals, and be ratified by the assent of the clergy and the acclamation of the people. The right of the emperor to confirm the choice was reserved in studiously vague language: 'saving due honour and reverence to Henry at this present time king, and destined, as it is hoped, to be emperor by the favour of God, even as we have granted this right to him and his successors, as many as shall personally obtain it from the apostolic see.' The Roman clergy were to have a prerogative right to the popedom, and Rome was to be the ordinary place of election; but, in default of a fit person being found within the Church of Rome, any stranger was eligible, and if from any cause the election could not take place inside the city, it might be held by the cardinals, clergy, and representatives of the faithful laity in any place which the cardinals might deem convenient, and the pope so elected, although not enthroned, should be entitled to exercise full papal authority. Appalling anathemas were pronounced on any who should violate this decree.

Decree respecting election to the Papacy

The council was the largest which had ever been gathered within the Lateran. One hundred and thirteen archbishops and bishops and a multitude of clergy were present, but full three-fourths of the prelates were Italian; the remainder came from Burgundy and France. Not one German bishop was present, and it is not surprising that some of the German clergy afterwards opposed a decree in framing which they had not been consulted. The council, in fact, simply ordained that the plan which had been actually followed in the election of Nicolas should be the rule for all future time.

The hapless Benedict had fled for refuge to the castle of Galeria; but after a short siege by the Norman troops of Nicolas, the garrison surrendered, on condition that Benedict's life was spared. Stripped of his pontifical robes, he was now led into the council by Hildebrand, and forced to read a confession of his misdeeds, which he did with many tears, his mother, with dishevelled hair, and other kinsfolk standing by weeping and wailing. Hildebrand cried aloud, 'Hearken, Romans! these be the deeds of the bishop whom ye have chosen.' The poor man was then degraded from his orders, and assigned a lodging in the church of St. Agnes, where he lived for about twenty years. Berengar also was compelled to read a recantation of his errors before the council, but as soon as he had returned to France he recanted his recantation.

Degradation of Benedict X.

Robert (surnamed Wiscard, or the Crafty), a son of Tancred of Hauteville by a second marriage, and Richard his brother-in-law, had entered Italy about six years before, and, after many wild adventures and hardships, had become the leaders of their countrymen there. Richard had wrested Capua from the Lombard lord, Landulf (1057). Robert, after the death of his half-brother, Humphrey, had become count of Apulia and Calabria, and was pushing on his conquests to the Straits of Messina. Hildebrand, soon after the election of Nicolas, hastened to Capua, and made a league with Richard, by which he swore fidelity to the Roman see,

NICOLAS II. AND ALEXANDER II. 49

on condition that he was recognised as Lord of Capua. Hildebrand asked and obtained immediate protection for Nicolas. Richard, with 300 horsemen, marched towards Rome, and on the way reduced all the strongholds of the refractory nobles: Tusculum, Mentana, Palestrina, and finally Galeria, as soon as Benedict was given up. At the same time Desiderius, abbot of Monte Cassino, who was made a cardinal, and apostolic vicar in Campania, Apulia, and Calabria, strengthened the alliance of the Papacy with the Normans by establishing friendly relations with Robert Wiscard.

Whilst Hildebrand had been busy in the south of Italy securing the bravest warriors of the age for the defence of the Papacy, Peter Damiani had been vigorously establishing papal authority in Lombardy. A fierce contest had long been raging in Milan between the clergy led by the archbishop, and a body of zealous, not to say fanatical, reformers who denounced clerical marriage as if it were a deadly sin. Anselm of Baggio, bishop of Lucca, Ariald, a deacon of humble birth, and Landulf, a Milanese nobleman, were the leaders of this party, contemptuously called the Patarines, or 'rag-bags,'[1] because they were joined by many of the lowest classes of the people. Amongst the Milanese clergy marriage was a fixed custom, for which they claimed the express sanction of St. Ambrose. The strife waxed hot and was not confined to words; violent and sanguinary tumults had broken out in the churches and the streets.

Peter Damiani sent as legate to Milan

Such was the condition of Milan when Peter Damiani, accompanied by Anselm of Lucca, appeared as legate

[1] 'Pataria' in the Milanese dialect is the word for rags.

of the pope to appease the strife. There could be no doubt which side the stern monk would support. His coming was hailed with joy by the Patarines, and struck the hearts of the clergy and the primate with terror and dismay. The indignation of the Milanese was excited when a synod was held in which they beheld their archbishop placed on the left hand of the legate, and Anselm of Lucca on his right. A riot broke out, in which Peter's life was in some danger; but he was not the man to quail, and archbishop Wido was not a man of great courage and determination. In the end Peter quelled disorder, proclaimed the supremacy of the Roman see, and exacted a repudiation of all customs condemned as heretical by Rome. The victory of the legate was crowned by the attendance of the archbishop and his suffragans, the bishops of Asti, Alba, Vercelli, Novara, Lodi, and Brescia at a synod in Rome, where they promised obedience to the papal see. The archbishop, who sat on the pope's right hand, was then re-invested with his archbishopric.

The result of Peter Damiani's mission in Milan was a great triumph for the Patarines, who gained a firmer footing throughout the whole of Lombardy. And the decrees passed in the Lateran Council, commanding all cathedral bodies to observe the rule of Chrodegang of Metz (which nearly assimilated the life of canons to that of monks), forbidding laymen to receive the Eucharist from the hands of a married priest, forbidding the clergy to receive any sacred office from lay hands, and the laity to exercise any jurisdiction over clerics, were hailed with delight by the severe reforming party, alike in Italy and Gaul. In Gaul, indeed, the policy of Hildebrand was supported, not only by the whole weight of the Clugniacs, but by one of the most distinguished men in rank and influence,—William, count of Poictiers and Anjou, and in Flanders by Baldwin, who was the friend of duke Godfrey, and after the death of Henry I. of France the guardian of the king's infant son.

But if the Papacy was backed by the moral force of public opinion in France, Aquitaine, Burgundy, Flanders, and northern Italy, it was to the Normans in the south of the peninsula that it looked for the material strength which only valour and skill in arms could supply. In the summer the pope, accompanied by Hildebrand, went to Monte Cassino, thence to Melfi in Apulia, where a great synod was held at which the decrees were proclaimed forbidding clerical marriage, especially common in that region, owing partly to Greek influence. More important was the formal removal of the ban which Leo IX. had imposed upon the Normans, and a confirmation of the alliance between the pope and the Norman chiefs Robert Wiscard and Richard of Capua. Both took the oath of fealty to the pope as suzerain, who now invested Robert with the dukedom of Apulia, Calabria, and Sicily, although the first two regions were not thoroughly conquered, and in Sicily he did not possess a foot of land. Richard was confirmed in the lordship of Capua, and henceforth the two brothers styled themselves, Robert, 'Duke,' and Richard, 'Lord, by the grace of God and Saint Peter.' Robert swore to defend all rights and possessions of the Holy See, to protect the pope, if canonically elected, in his person and property, and on all the lands held of him

Visit of the pope to Apulia, 1059

to pay an annual tribute of twelve pence for every yoke of oxen.

As suzerain of the Normans, as protector of the Patarines, as the ally of duke Godfrey and Beatrice, the pope stood in the centre of all national life in Italy. The castles of the tyrannical nobles were broken down, the stiff neck of the Lombard bull was bent beneath the papal yoke; the affairs of the whole peninsula once more revolved round Rome as their pivot. Outside Italy the Papacy could reckon on moral support at least in Gaul, and from the weak government in Germany no serious resistance could be apprehended.

Strength of the pope's position

After a visit to Benevento, where he held a synod, the pope returned to Florence, of which he held the bishopric to the end of his life; and here he spent most of his time, only visiting Rome at Easter to preside in the great synods.

Hildebrand about this time was made archdeacon. He became more than ever the moving spring of all business in Rome; and he now lived in such constant intercourse with men of the world, and assumed so much secular grandeur in his dress, retinue, and general style of living, as to shock some of his more ascetic friends, especially Peter Damiani. There is no more striking proof of the force of Hildebrand's commanding genius than the sway which he exercised over this remarkable man. Peter longed to resign his bishopric and return to his beloved retreat at Monte Avellana, yet dared not disobey the command of Hildebrand to stay where he was; and although he disapproved of many things which Hilde-

Hildebrand made archdeacon

His relations to Peter Damiani

brand did, and never shrank from expressing his disapproval, yet he always undertook the tasks assigned to him. He loved yet feared him almost equally, and grimly called him his 'holy Satan.' 'Thy will,' he said, 'has ever been for me a command—evil yet lawful. Would that I had always served God and St. Peter as faithfully as I have striven to do thy behests.'

The election of an Italian pope, the decree of the Lateran Council vesting the right of election in the cardinals with a very ambiguous reservation of imperial rights, and the manifest aim of Hildebrand to raise the Papacy into a great central independent power, excited considerable suspicion at the German court and amongst the German clergy. Anno, archbishop of Cöln, an astute and ambitious man, clearly saw what a loss of wealth and influence, especially in Italy, would be incurred by the German Church if the popes were henceforth to be Italians elected by Italians. He summoned a synod of bishops (1059 or 1060) in which resolutions were passed pronouncing Nicolas disqualified for his office by reason of a stain on his birth, forbidding his name to be mentioned in the public prayers, and even threatening him with deposition. Anno seems to have succeeded in prejudicing the German court, if not the empress Agnes herself, against the Hildebrandists. Cardinal Stephen, having been despatched to transact some business with the empress, was denied admission, and after waiting five days returned with his errand unaccomplished.

Relations of Germany and the Pope

The unfriendly attitude of the German court and clergy towards the pope revived the courage of the hostile party in Lombardy, and perhaps stimulated the nobles near Rome to fresh deeds of lawlessness. Ealdred, archbishop of York, Tostig, earl of Northumberland, and the bishops of Wells and Hereford, who visited Rome (Easter, 1061) to obtain a confirmation of privileges for the new abbey at Westminster, were plundered on their return at Sutri by count Girard of Galeria. They went back to Rome, and Tostig bluntly told the pope that before he presumed to rule the world he ought to maintain order in his own dominions. They received compensation for their losses, and Ealdred now got the pallium which the pope had formerly refused because he held the see of Worcester with his archbishopric. At the synod held just afterwards, Girard was excommunicated, and at the same time the decree respecting papal elections was confirmed.

It was soon to be proved whether this decree could be enforced, for on July 27 the pope died. His pontificate was important rather from the events which occurred in it than from the character of the man. He played his part with dignity, but the head which guided his actions was the head of Hildebrand.

Death of Nicolas II. 1061

As soon as the death of the pope was announced in Rome the nobles sent the count Girard (the excommunicated robber) and the abbot of St. Gregory on the Cœlian to the German court, bearing the insignia of the patriciate for the young king, with a request that a nomination might be made to the vacant papal chair. Hildebrand and his party waited two months before taking a decisive step. Probably they were trying to ascertain whether they could depend on the support of duke Godfrey and the Normans in the threefold contest which now threatened them—with the Roman nobility, the German imperialists, and the faction in Lombardy which was opposed to reform.

At length they resolved to abide by the decree of the Lateran Council. The cardinals met on October 1 and elected Anselm of Baggio, the bishop of Lucca. Anselm belonged to a distinguished family in Milan; he had been one of the earlier scholars of Lanfranc at Bec, and on his return from that seat of learning he had preached vehemently at Milan against simony and the marriage of the clergy. Henry III. made him one of his chaplains, and in 1056 appointed him to the bishopric of Lucca. He was on terms of friendly intimacy with duke Godfrey, and although he was a firm supporter of Hildebrand and the reformers, he seemed well fitted by his Lombard origin and his former connexion with the German court, to knit together all parties in the Church. These hopes, however, were to be disappointed. The moment was come for the Normans to make good their character as defenders of the Holy See. Under the protection of Richard of Capua and his followers, Anselm, who took the name of Alexander II., was enthroned by night in the church of St. Peter ad Vincula and conducted to the Lateran palace, where his first act was to administer the oath of fealty to the Norman leader. The introduction of Norman troops was unpopular in Rome. The election without any reference to the royal court gave great offence in Germany, and the Lombard bishops were incensed at the elevation of such a warm supporter of the Patarines. They held a meeting under the presidency of Wibert of Parma, the imperial chancellor, and passed a resolution that they would not recognise anyone as pope who was not chosen from their party. They also sent envoys to the empress, to represent that by the decree of pope Nicolas II. the election of a pope must be confirmed by the agent of the emperor. Agnes was a weak, pliable woman: weary of the world, she had recently decided to take the veil and retire from the cares and vexations of public life, and responsibilities for which she felt herself unfitted. But she could see plainly enough that unless some prompt step was taken Rome and Italy would slip out of the reach of German control. The strength and grandeur of the late emperor's position had been immensely enhanced by the distinguished part which he had played in the appointment of the popes, and in the work of ecclesiastical reform; but now the reformed Papacy was acting in complete independence of the Empire, and in close alliance with duke Godfrey and the Normans, who had been the most formidable enemies of Henry III.

Discontent in Lombardy and Germany

A synod was summoned to meet at Basel on October 28, 1061. The empress and young Henry were present, with the envoys from Rome, and a large number of bishops from Germany and Lombardy. Having invested Henry with the insignia of the patriciate, the synod annulled the election of Alexander as irregular, and, through the influence of the Lombard prelates, elected Cadalus, bishop of Parma, to take the place of the usurper.

Synod at Basel elects Cadalus, bishop of Parma

Cadalus belonged to a wealthy family of Verona, and had been bishop of Parma for nearly twenty years.

On the first visit of Henry III. to Italy he had attracted the notice of the emperor, and he retained his favour although he never sympathised with the zeal of Henry's popes for the reformation of the Church. He became, in fact, the head of the opposition to the Patarines, and at the synods of Pavia (1049), Mantua (1052), and Florence (1055) accusations of simony were made against him, which, had they been pressed, might have led to his deposition.

The appointment of Cadalus, who took the name of Honorius II., was bad policy for the interests of the empress and her son, for as an Italian he was distasteful to the Germans, and to the whole body of reformers he was odious. Peter Damiani addressed a letter to him filled with the fiercest denunciations ever hurled by the Hebrew prophets against the wicked and profane. Nothing daunted, however, the anti-pope made preparations for entering Rome early in the year 1062. Benzo, bishop of Alba, a clever, eloquent man, and a virulent adversary of the Hildebrandists, was sent in advance, and by a lavish expenditure of money and oratory succeeded in forming a large party for Cadalus inside the city. On one occasion when he was haranguing the people in a hippodrome Alexander appeared on horseback with his retinue. 'Away, leper! Out, wretch! Begone, hateful one!' cried the bishop of Alba, and the pope was forced to retreat amidst the abuse and derision of the mob. Richard of Capua had quitted Rome to quell an insurrection at Capua. Hildebrand and Alexander with difficulty raised some irregular troops; but their raw levies were no match for the forces of the anti-pope, who arrived in April outside the walls of Rome, supported by many of the counts of the Campagna, with Girard of Galeria at their head. An engagement took place in which Alexander's men were worsted, and Cadalus got possession of the precincts of St. Peter's. The exertions of Hildebrand, however, with the aid of his wealthy friend Leo, son of the converted Jew, Benedict, raised more troops, who succeeded in dislodging Cadalus from his position. He fixed his camp near Tusculum, where he could rely on the support of the counts and prepare for another attack upon Rome. An exceedingly bitter, but dismal and desponding, letter of Peter Damiani's proves that he thought the cause of Alexander almost hopeless, when the aspect of affairs was suddenly changed by the arrival before Rome of duke Godfrey with an overwhelming body of troops. His arrival, however, did not fulfil the worst fears of Cadalus or the highest hopes of Hildebrand and Alexander. He merely commanded the two popes to retire from Rome to their episcopal sees: Alexander to Lucca, Honorius to Parma, and there await the decision of the king upon their rival claims. The nature of this decision was determined by a revolution which had taken place in Germany.

A struggle for the possession of Rome

CHAPTER VI.

RELATIONS OF GERMANY TO THE PAPACY DURING THE MINORITY OF HENRY IV. 1056–66.

WHILST Hildebrand had been steadily building up the papacy into a strong central power, the German king-
<small>Condition of Germany, 1056–1062</small> dom had been weakened by internal strife. It would have been scarcely possible for any woman, however able, successfully to govern so large a territory parcelled out amongst feudal lords of various ranks—dukes, counts, margraves—all jealous of each other, and perpetually quarrelling for precedence. But the empress-mother was unfitted by her character, as well as her sex, for such a task. She was religious and well-intentioned, but weak of will. The court was beset with intrigues, and the empress hearkened first to one counsellor and then to another. Woman-like she had her favourites, who, on account of this influence, were the objects both of flattery and detestation. Nothing, it was said, could be obtained at court except through gold or favour.

The increasing opulence and power of the bishops had excited the envy of the lay nobles, and they thought that the weak regency was an opportunity for humbling them. The high-born and ambitious Adalbert, archbishop of Bremen, was one of the most distinguished prelates, and most devoted to the royal family. His episcopal lands were constantly harried by Ordulf, duke of Saxony, who heeded neither the excommunications of the primate nor the commands of the empress. The best means of escape which Adalbert could devise was to invest Herman, the brother of Ordulf, with a large portion of episcopal territory, on condition of his acting as a guardian of the see.

Anno of Cöln, not high-born, but not less ambitious, was involved in similar strife with the Palsgrave, Henry, but succeeded in defeating him. The Palsgrave died mad, and his son was made a vassal of the see.

The prelate who had by far the greatest influence with the empress was Henry, bishop of Augsburg, and he consequently incurred peculiar hatred. Base slanders respecting their intimacy were circulated, which, however groundless, served the turn of the malicious. In short the envy and discontent of the nobles constantly increased. They rarely attended court, frequently held secret meetings, and fomented disaffection amongst the people. The chief leaders of the malcontents were archbishop Anno, Otto of Nordheim, who had been recently made duke of Bavaria, and count Ecbert of Brunswick, a kinsman of the king. At last a plot was formed by these three for getting Henry, now twelve years old, out of his mother's power, and taking the administration of the kingdom into their own hands.

The empress and her son spent the beginning of the year 1062 at Goslar in Saxony, accompanied by the obnoxious bishop of Augsburg. In March they moved to Paderborn. Easter Day (March 31st) was spent at Utrecht. After the festival they went with a small retinue to a palace at St. Suitberth's on the Rhine, a place now called Kaiserswerth, situated between Duisberg and Düsseldorf. It was then an island, but by an alteration in the course of the stream it has been joined to the right bank of the river. One day, in the month of May, the three conspirators appeared with a numerous company as if to pay a friendly visit. They were received without suspicion and hospitably entertained. After dinner the archbishop persuaded the young king to go and see his barge, which was sumptuously fitted up; but no sooner was the child on board than the crew pushed off and rowed with all their might up the stream. The terrified boy flung himself overboard, but the count Ecbert plunged in after him and rescued him, after great exertions, at the peril of his own life. The child was soothed with kind words, and the barge proceeded to Cöln, but an indignant crowd followed it along the shore and poured forth execrations on the perpetrators of a deed so treacherous, treasonable, and cruel. The empress passionately bewailed the loss of her son, but took no steps to recover him, and after a time was publicly reconciled to Anno. She was, indeed, well content to be relieved from the burden of government which she was ill fitted to bear, and longed to retire into a monastery, a wish which she not long afterwards gratified. There is no evidence that duke Godfrey was directly concerned in the plot for the abduction of the king, yet the conspirators could hardly have ventured upon the deed without the tacit consent at least of so powerful a man, and the whole of the Hildebrandine party did not scruple to take advantage of the event. Peter Damiani, in a complimentary letter to the archbishop, likens him to Jehoiada, the high priest, the guardian, and instructor of the young

Abduction of the young king, 1062

king Joash; a very unfortunate illustration, for the gentle and pious empress was no counterpart of Athaliah, while Henry had neither love nor respect for Anno, by whom his education and moral training were shamefully neglected. 'He lived,' as one of the annalists says, 'unhappily, because he lived as he pleased.' He was allowed to dissipate his time in frivolous amusements. His abilities were good, but they were not cultivated; his passions were strong, and he was not taught to control them.

An assembly of nobles held at Cöln, probably about Whitsuntide (1062), decided that the guardianship of the king and the chief administration of affairs should devolve on the bishop in whose diocese the king was for the time being resident. Anno, however, took good care that these bishops should be such as were friendly to himself, and foremost amongst them were Gunther of Bamberg and Siegfried of Mainz.

On October 28 the council was held in Augsburg which was to decide between the claims of the contending popes. There could be little doubt what that decision would be. The recognition of Alexander would be an easy price for Anno to pay the Hildebrandine party for their consent to a deed which made him and his confederates the virtual rulers of the kingdom.

<small>Council of Augsburg, 1062</small>

Of the proceedings at the council we have no detailed account. Perhaps the necessity of debate was thought to be superseded by the production of an imaginary dialogue, composed by Peter Damiani, between the advocates of the king and of the Roman Church. The advocate of the Church

<small>Dialogue composed by Peter Damiani</small>

does not deny the ordinary right of the German king to confirm the election of a pope, but concludes that, as a matter of fact, many popes had been elected without this confirmation, and that the rule, like all others, must sometimes yield to necessity. In the present case delay had been dangerous: the king was too young to exercise an independent judgment; the Roman Church was his spiritual mother; it was for her to direct his choice during his tender years, and when her own legate, a cardinal of high rank and irreproachable character, had been refused admission to the court, while count Girard, an excommunicated robber, had been allowed to represent the Roman nobles, it was impossible for the cardinals to respect the discretion of the German court. It was true that a curse was pronounced upon any who should violate the decree of the Lateran Council which reserved the royal rights in papal elections, but God would absolve those who had broken it only out of love for Him and His Church, for even God Himself did not always fulfil His promises or execute His threats.

By these arguments, which are worked out with no little ingenuity and some sophistry, the advocate of the king at last confesses himself vanquished. And the whole disputation concludes with a pious prayer that, as the kingly and priestly offices were combined in the one Mediator between God and man, so henceforth there might be an indissoluble union between the spiritual and temporal heads of the human race on earth, the king being recognised in the pontiff, and the pontiff in the king. The intrinsic superiority, however, of the sacerdotal to the royal office is carefully maintained. The pope is the father, the king is his dearly beloved son: the father has paternal rights to assert, the son has filial duties to perform.

The council, however much it may have been convinced, or predetermined, in favour of Alexander, acted with caution. The pope had been accused of simony, and of intrigues with the Normans, as well as of irregularity in his election. The council therefore resolved to send an envoy to Italy, to investigate these charges, and, if satisfied of Alexander's innocence, to conduct him to Rome, there to discharge the papal office until a general council should be held in Italy. The envoy was Anno's nephew, Burchard, bishop of Halberstadt. He pronounced Alexander guiltless, conducted him to Rome (January, 1063), and returned to Germany with the pallium as a reward of his services.

The partisans of the anti-pope still held the castle of St. Angelo, but for the present his cause was lost; a complete reconciliation had been effected between the German hierarchy and the Hildebrandists; the right of the king to control the papal election had been practically surrendered, the rights of the cardinals to make a free choice had been practically acknowledged. These concessions laid the foundation of infinite future troubles, but the immediate result was conducive to peace, and to Anno personally it was a great triumph. He became the chief personage in the realm. Siegfried of Mainz subsided into comparative insignificance; Adalbert of Bremen was the only serious rival of his power.

The guardianship of the king and the administration of affairs was, in fact, divided between the archbishops of Cöln and Bremen. Both were men of resolute will and lofty ambition. The aim of Anno was to make

Cöln the ecclesiastical metropolis of all Germany; the design of Adalbert was to convert his see into a kind of northern patriarchate, with an extensive jurisdiction over Scandinavian countries. Both prelates were sumptuous in their style of living, energetic in their labours, and munificent in their gifts; they lavished bounties on the poor, they founded or enriched monasteries, they built churches, they organised missions. But they were not content with the exercise of spiritual powers. Partly by means of royal grants, partly through bribery and intrigue, they became feudal suzerains within their dioceses, they obtained bishoprics for their relations and partisans, and secured temporal rights for them similar to their own.

In other respects the two prelates were unlike each other. Anno, a man of humble birth, assumed a haughty tone towards men of rank; to inferiors he was affable and condescending. The high-born Adalbert, on the other hand, was harsh and overbearing to men of low rank, but his vanity made him very susceptible to flattery, and he was surrounded by a crowd of parasites, on whom he showered favours and gifts with a prodigal hand. He was a thorough courtier with a genuine reverence for the royal majesty; naturally, therefore, he became the favourite guardian of the young king, who looked upon him as an indulgent friend, while he regarded Anno rather as a despotic schoolmaster. Neither of them, however, trained the boy so as to fit him for the high and responsible position to which he was heir; he was never taught that most important of all lessons for anyone who has to govern others—how to govern himself. His favourite companion as he grew up was the count Werner, a hot-headed young man. He and archbishop Adalbert managed the king; no secular or ecclesiastical office could be obtained except through them, and their favour could only be bought by a large expenditure of money.

After Easter (1063), pope Alexander held a synod in Rome attended by more than a hundred bishops. Position of the rival popes. The decrees against simony and the marriage of the clergy were renewed, and the anti-pope was anathematised, as guilty of simony and violence. Cadalus held a counter-synod at Parma, in which Alexander was anathematised as having been irregularly elected; but the position of the anti-pope was very precarious. The bishops of Lombardy and the archbishop of Ravenna stood by him, but he could not reckon on any support from Germany. In Rome he could command a party as long as his money lasted, but fierce brawls often broke out in the streets between his partisans and Alexander's. He only held the Leonine city for a time, and when he was driven out of that, nothing remained to him but the castle of St. Angelo, which was in the hands of Cencius, one of the bitterest opponents of Hildebrand.

In October, Peter Damiani wrote to Anno urging that the general council, at which the claims of the rival popes were to be decided, should be held as soon as possible; and soon after Christmas summonses were issued for the council to be held at Mantua in the coming spring. Alexander and Hildebrand were excessively displeased at this step on the part of Peter, and Hildebrand wrote to him a bitter letter of reproof. The popularity of the anti-pope was fast diminishing as his exchequer began to fail, and the triumph of Alexander would be impaired by the meeting of a council to discuss his claims as if they were still in dispute. There was no help for it, however;—the council was called, Alexander attended it with Hildebrand and Peter Damiani, while Cadalus sulkily retired to Aqua Nigra near Cremona, because the place of precedence was not guaranteed to him beforehand.

The council was opened in the cathedral of Mantua on May 31. After high mass Alexander made an address upon the distracted condition of Christendom. Anno then stated the charges which were made against him—the irregularity of his election, and his alleged intrigues with the Normans. Alexander defended himself on oath. The council declared itself satisfied, and acknowledged him as lawful pope; a Te Deum was sung, Cadalus was anathematised. Some of his adherents raised a tumult the next day in the town, and burst into the assembly with drawn swords, but they were quelled by the appearance of the countess Beatrice with a body of armed followers.

Council of Mantua, 1064.

Alexander II. declared pope.

As soon as the king entered his fifteenth year the ceremony of girding him with a sword was performed at Worms, March 29. Duke Godfrey of Lotharingia carried his shield, and Eberhard, archbishop of Trier, bound the sword upon him. The ceremony had been arranged at the earliest possible opportunity by archbishop Adalbert, as it implied that the youth was no longer under tutors and governors, and that the office of Anno then came to an end. We are told that, had he not been restrained by his mother,

Henry IV. begins to reign, 1065.

he would have proved his sword upon the body of the archbishop, whom he had never forgiven for the treacherous deed at Kaiserswerth.

It was indeed a sad inheritance to which the young king succeeded. The political fabric which his father had built up in Germany with so much toil and care, was crumbling to pieces; the royal power was sapped by the encroachments of a proud and selfish feudal aristocracy; the imperial crown had yet to be obtained, and the imperial authority, meanwhile, was in abeyance; in Italy the name of duke Godfrey commanded more respect and reverence than the king's, and if the goodwill of Hildebrand and Alexander had been secured, it was by the sacrifice of the king's claim to a voice in the election of the pope.

To many there seemed to be urgent need, on all grounds, that the king should visit Italy without delay, to receive the imperial crown. For the removal of Anno from power had revived the hopes of the anti-pope, who still had a strong party in Lombardy, and had never renounced his pretensions, issuing decrees, granting privileges, and assuming all the customary pomp of popes. The increasing power of the Normans also, and their peculiar relations to the Papacy, were a kind of menace to imperial authority. Peter Damiani looked upon the visit of the king as the only hope of healing the schism in the Church, and wrote a letter to him passionately entreating him to come and do his duty as the protector of his spiritual mother. Duke Godfrey, also, and Anno shared his view, and began to make preparations for the expedition. It seemed on the eve of being accomplished;

Visit of the king to Italy proposed but frustrated

but it was not to be. Adalbert was opposed to the design, from jealousy of Anno and Godfrey; Hildebrand and the pope were opposed to it because their great aim was to make the Papacy an independent centre of power. Hence the projected visit was put off from the spring to the autumn, and from the autumn to a more convenient season which never came. Twelve years were to pass before Henry crossed the Alps, and then he was to go, not in royal state, to receive the imperial crown, but in penitential guise, to crave release from excommunication, lest the crown which he already had should be taken away from him.

CHAPTER VII.

THE FIRST SIX YEARS OF THE REIGN OF HENRY IV.
1066–72.

THE power of archbishop Adalbert reached its meridian in the summer of the year 1065. He and the young count Werner were constantly about the king, and disposed of all offices, secular and ecclesiastical, according to their own will and pleasure. The vanity, avarice, and ambition of the primate grew with prosperity, and his unpopularity naturally increased in the same proportion. On Bremen he bestowed great gifts and privileges, and in the magnificence of its buildings the city might be compared with Cöln, but the cathedral chapter was heavily taxed to support the archbishop's costly undertakings, and his rare visits to his see were dreaded rather than welcomed;

because they were always accompanied by a demand for money. Nevertheless, he lived on unconscious of danger, surrounded by his parasites, who extolled him as the patriarch of the North, and predicted that he would one day be pope. But the storm-clouds had been piling up and were soon to burst. Adalbert maintained that the king had absolute rights over the royal abbeys, and in the spring of 1065 he persuaded Henry to let him seize the revenues of Lorsch and Corbey, and tried to bribe Anno into acquiescence by promising to get the rich abbey of Malmedy for him. But the houses of Lorsch and Corbey obstinately and successfully resisted these acts of spoliation; and the indignation and disgust of the nobles became so strong that they forgot for a time their personal jealousies in a determination to put down Adalbert. At a diet which met at Tribur in January, 1066, and was attended by archbishops Anno and Siegfried, Otto, count of Bavaria, Rudolf of Swabia, and many other nobles and prelates, the king was offered the choice between banishing the archbishop of Bremen or abdicating the throne. He tried to evade the hard alternatives, and Adalbert formed a plan for their escape by night, but it was detected and frustrated. He himself, however, contrived to fly from Tribur on the following night, and made his way to Bremen; leaving the king to confront the nobles as best he might. Henry was, in fact, as much a prisoner in their hands as on the day of Kaiserswerth; but he was no longer a child, and he had no intention of submitting tamely to anyone, least of all to Anno and his associates.

Nevertheless for the next three years (1066–1069) the administration of affairs was conducted mainly by the

bishops in a kind of rotation, the acting bishop being elected by the nobles and the archbishops, and sub-
<small>Relation of the German prelates to the Papacy</small> ject to their supervision. The primates and the nobles seem to have kept on good terms with Rome. A bull of Alexander's ratifying Anno's foundation of the monastery of Siegburg is full of compliments to the archbishop. Siegfried of Mainz also obtained the pallium, and in an obsequious letter to Alexander, in the spring of 1066, he entirely concedes the right of the pope to bestow both the royal and imperial crowns. 'As the crown of our kingdom and the diadem of the whole Roman Empire has been given by St. Peter into thy hands, we beseech thee ever to have our lord King Henry in good remembrance; and as thou hast hitherto upheld him with thy counsel and deeds, so we pray thee to continue to uphold him with apostolic constancy even to the time of his imperial coronation.'

Certainly Hildebrand could not have wished for a more positive recognition than this of the papal right to set up and depose kings; and it is clear that from this date the German nobles, having yielded to the Roman Church the right of electing the pope, were extremely anxious to obtain from the pope the imperial crown for their king. Unless this was gained it was obvious that the position of the pope as an independent power in Italy would be immensely strengthened, to the detriment of German influence.

Under the administration of the nobles a stop was put to the lavish waste of royal property, and the rich abbeys which had been bestowed on Adalbert were surrendered. Anno, however, with characteristic craft, kept possession of Stablo and Malmedy. The fall of

Adalbert and the death of count Werner, who was killed in a private brawl, enabled him to become again for a short time the most commanding figure in the state. In the presence of Anno in the council the young king sat petrified and mute, whilst the archbishop spoke for him. But this season of submission was short-lived. Henry detested Anno, and his proud and passionate spirit fretted under the galling yoke of subjection to the nobles, although from prudence or fear he dissembled his feelings for a time.

The first open quarrel was about his marriage with Bertha, to whom he had been betrothed ten years. The nobles insisted that it should now take place. Bertha was young and beautiful, of amiable disposition and irreproachable character; but Henry had contracted licentious habits, and he fancied that Bertha, who had been brought up in Germany, was the mere nursling and tool of his tyrannical guardians. He sullenly consented to the marriage, which was celebrated on July 13; but he refused to live with his wife, and three years later, in a diet held at Worms (Whitsuntide 1069), he boldly declared his intention to be divorced. He had secretly informed Siegfried of Mainz of this determination, and the crafty primate had promised to support him, on condition that the king would help him to force some refractory tithe-payers in Thuringia to pay their dues.

Marriage of Henry IV., 1066

He seeks a divorce

The nobles were dismayed at the announcement made by Henry. He did not, indeed, bring any accusation against his poor blameless wife, but simply declared that his aversion to her was invincible. The council postponed a decision on the matter to another diet, to be held in the autumn at Mainz, and meanwhile the opinion of the Pope upon the question was to be obtained.

During the summer Henry was occupied in putting down a rebellion of the margrave Dedi, who tried to seize the Thuringian fiefs belonging to archbishop Siegfried and the king. Dedi had reckoned on the support of the Thuringians, but he was disappointed. Alarmed at the size of the force which Henry had mustered, the Thuringians joined his side, and by their aid the rebellion of the margrave was crushed, notwithstanding which Henry compelled them to pay the disputed tithes to the archbishop of Mainz.

<small>Suppresses a rebellion of the margrave Dedi</small>

The vigour and promptness with which he had acted in these affairs raised the reputation of the king; and the nobles could no longer doubt that they had to deal with an able and strong-willed sovereign. Henry, perhaps, hoped that he should now be able to have his way about the divorce; but on his journey to Mainz he heard with dismay that Peter Damiani was going to attend it as papal legate. He knew what he had to expect from such an austere upholder of ecclesiastical discipline. At first he withdrew into Saxony; then, yielding to the entreaties of the nobles, he determined to face his fate, but shifted the place of assembly from Mainz to Frankfurt.

The archbishop of Mainz had been deputed by the council at Worms to represent the king's case at Rome. He had long wished to get a papal decision in favour of his claims to the Thuringian tithes, and he thought he saw his opportunity; he

<small>Council of Frankfurt, 1069</small>

hoped to get the tithe dispute settled by legatine authority, and to evade all responsibility in the matter of the king's divorce. But he was grievously deceived. Peter Damiani, in the Council of Frankfurt, announced that if the king put away his innocent wife, the pope would inflict upon him the severest penalties of the Church, and withhold the imperial crown. The tithe question was not settled, and Siegfried was threatened with deprivation if he dared any more to countenance the wicked intentions of the king.

The archbishop and the nobles urged Henry to yield, dwelling more especially upon the great mischief which might be done to the kingdom by the powerful kinsfolk of the queen in Burgundy and Italy. At last Henry gave way; he invited the queen to meet him at Goslar; he not only conquered his repugnance, but became sincerely attached to her, and in the bitter calamities and distresses of his afterlife, she was his constant companion and comforter. Their first child, Conrad, was born in August of the year 1071.

The king consents to live with his wife

Peter Damiani took back a favourable report of the young king to Rome; but he drew the darkest picture of the shameless licentiousness of the German nobility, and of the corruption of the Church. The decrees against simony and clerical marriage were everywhere notoriously defied. Hildebrand and the pope resolved to make examples of offenders in the highest rank. Archbishops Siegfried and Anno, and Herman, bishop of Bamberg, were summoned to the Easter synod at Rome (1070), to answer in person the charge of simony. Their guilt

German bishops humbled at Rome

FIRST SIX YEARS OF THE REIGN OF HENRY IV. 75

was clearly proved: money had been taken for ordination, benefices had been bought and sold. The bishop of Bamberg, indeed, had actually bought his bishopric. These great prelates were thoroughly humbled; Siegfried even offered to resign his dignity and retire into a monastery. But it suited the policy of the pope and his advisers better to permit them to retain their offices, under a promise on oath of amendment, and of submissive obedience to the Roman See. On their return to Germany they edified the world by the spectacle of their extreme piety, and especially their devotion to the monastic orders. Siegfried went into retreat at Clugny; Anno performed the menial offices of a servitor in the house which he had founded at Siegburg. Herman induced a count of the same name to found a monastery at Banz, and removed secular canons for monks in his own cathedral at Bamberg. The prelates, however, who had returned from Rome so seriously discredited, could no longer presume to be the directors of the king, and Adalbert of Bremen once more emerged from obscurity, and nearly recovered his old position at court.

The humiliation of the great bishops nearly coincided with the death of the most powerful noble in the Empire, duke Godfrey of Lotharingia. Godfrey was a man who had been feared by all and trusted by few. The Hildebrandists owed much to his support, yet there were times when his dealings with the Normans and the anti-pope had filled them with apprehension and suspicion. Godfrey surnamed 'hunchback,' his son by his first marriage, had wedded Matilda the daughter of his widow Beatrice by her

<small>Death of duke Godfrey, Christmas 1069</small>

first marriage. He took the title of count of Tuscany and duke of Spoleto, but he cared little for his wife or his Italian possessions, which he left almost entirely to the management of Matilda and her mother. They were intensely devoted to the cause of the pope and Hildebrand, and thus the death of the elder Godfrey, although it removed one who might at any time be dangerous to the German throne, also weakened the hold of Germany on Italy and the pope. At the same time the German kingdom itself began to be distracted by the internal strifes and wars from which it was never delivered during the whole reign of Henry IV. When he took the government into his own hands, a twofold task lay before him: to enforce the supremacy of the crown over the nobles, and to reduce the Saxons, who had never been thoroughly subjugated, to submission.

In the summer of 1070, Otto, duke of Bavaria, perhaps the most powerful of the nobles next to duke Godfrey, was accused of treasonable designs. It is hard to say how much truth there was in the charge: many circumstances were suspicious, but he had bitter enemies at court, and he had been concerned in the abduction of the king at Kaiserswerth; he was pronounced guilty by a council of Saxon nobles, and his lands were forfeited to the crown. After resisting in arms for a year, Otto surrendered and was leniently dealt with, being released after a brief imprisonment and having most of his lands restored to him, but not his duchy.

Rebellion of Otto of Bavaria

The relations, however, between Henry and his nobles became more and more strained; he disliked and distrusted them, and bestowed the chief offices of state upon his own personal friends, many of them nowise distinguished by birth or territorial wealth. The people complained of the insolence and oppression of these creatures of the crown; and the old nobility resented the intrusion of adventurers into positions to which they deemed themselves to have a prescriptive right. When the king began a system of castle-building in Saxony and Thuringia, and filled the castles with armed garrisons, alarm was added to indignation. Rudolf, duke of Swabia, who had married a sister of queen Bertha, became the leader of a strong party of disaffected nobles, who sullenly held aloof from court and were ready to excite or lead rebellion in any part of the kingdom. The death of archbishop Adalbert in 1072, and the retirement of Anno, in shame and disgust, from all active share in state affairs, removed the last counsellors of the old school who had retained any influence over the king. Men knew not whither his unbridled impulses would hurry him, and there was a general feeling of uneasiness and vague apprehension.

CHAPTER VIII.

STATE OF THE CHURCH IN ITALY. SURVEY OF THE POSITION OF THE PAPACY IN EUROPE AT THE DEATH OF ALEXANDER II. 1073.

WHILST the German kingdom was being weakened by internal dissensions Hildebrand had been consolidating the papal power in Italy; striving to heal the schism in the Church in Lombardy, to cement the friendship with Beatrice and Matilda of Tuscany, and to preserve the alliance with the Normans in Apulia.

In Milan the Patarines, under Ariald and Landulf, seemed to have secured the submission of the Church to Rome; but as soon as Cadalus was set up as anti-pope, archbishop Wido and many of the clergy went over to his side. In 1065 Landulf died, but his brother Erlembald, a warlike knight and a religious enthusiast, took his place as leader of the Patarines. If his brother had chastised the peccant clergy with whips, he was resolved to chastise them with scorpions: the married men were searched out and punished with the most merciless severity. Archbishop Wido excommunicated Ariald and Erlembald, but the latter appealed to Rome early in 1066, and came back armed with a consecrated banner, and a bull excommunicating the archbishop. For a time he and Ariald carried all before them, but a rash attempt to alter the old Ambrosian Use, which the Milanese held in peculiar veneration, provoked a fierce tumult. Ariald fled for refuge to Legnano, where he was cruelly murdered. Erlembald was forced to quit the city, and the archbishop and his partisans returned. The cause of the Patarines, however, was popular with the country folk; and the death of Ariald only irritated the party to fresh exertions. Erlembald soon raised a force with which he regained possession of the city, and the old oaths, so often taken, so often broken, pledging the clergy to renounce simony and marriage, and the laity to persecute simoniacal or married priests even to death, were once more administered.

In the year 1068 Wido, weary of strife, resigned the

archbishopric of Milan. Erlembald was instructed by Hildebrand to take care that a canonical election was made by the clergy and people, with the assent of the pope, and without investiture by the German king.

Meanwhile, however, Wido had sent Godfrey, a subdeacon, a Milanese of good family, to the German court with the ring and staff, recommending him as his successor, and offering a handsome sum to the king if he acceded to the recommendation. Henry imprudently invested him, but the people and clergy of Milan refused to accept him, and the pope excommunicated both Godfrey and the archbishop. The vacillating Wido apologised, did penance, and resumed his office; while Godfrey retired to his family castle at Castiglione.

In August 1071 archbishop Wido died. Then the strife began again. There was a general agreement that the election should be made by the canons of the cathedral, but should it be confirmed by the king or by the pope? that was the question. Erlembald strove hard to get it settled in favour of the pope, but there was a strong party, chiefly of the upper ranks, in Milan, who upheld the right of the king. Six months were consumed in debate and negotiation. At length Erlembald deemed himself strong enough to carry the election: on January 6, 1072, a motley multitude of laymen and clerics, brought together from the neighbouring towns as well as from Milan, elected a young deacon named Atto, not connected with the cathedral, and otherwise of no distinction. The citizens of Milan were enraged at the appointment: they dragged the wretched Atto from the palace to the church of St. Mary, and forced him to mount the pulpit and there repudiate his own election. The pope and Hildebrand, however, pronounced his election valid, and his repudiation of it worthless. Erlembald was plentifully supplied with money from Rome and had a strong armed force at his back, and with the help of these two potent instruments—gold and iron—he remained master of Milan. In Piacenza also and Cremona the Patarine party had the upper hand; but the crown-ing mercy for the cause of Alexander was the death of Cadalus, the anti-pope (Honorius II.), which occurred early in the year.

<small>Death of the anti-pope Honorius II., January, 1072</small>

The ten years' schism had ended distinctly to the advantage of the Hildebrandists. The strength of the Lombard opposition was broken; the power of the German king was contracted; many of the Italian cities were grateful to Rome for having put a check upon the despotic rule of the bishops and their captains.

<small>Survey of the Papal position.
i. In Lombardy</small>

And if we take a wider survey we see the power of Rome taking deeper root in every part of Western Europe. In Southern Italy, no doubt, the cupidity and ambition of the Normans were often a source of anxiety to the pope; and, as a check upon their advances northwards, Hildebrand sometimes deemed it prudent to give some support to a rebellious Norman vassal or to the remnants of Lombard power in the neighbourhood of Benevento. On the other hand, blended with a spirit of proud independence and daring enterprise in the Norman leaders, there was a singular vein of religious sentiment. The conquerors had craved absolution from Leo IX., and acknowledged him as their suzerain

THE POSITION OF THE PAPACY IN EUROPE

on the very field where they had defeated his army.[1] They received the pope with profound respect whenever he visited them, and they rigorously enforced the papal decrees against simony and clerical marriage within their dominions. Robert Wiscard divorced himself from his wife Alberada, on religious scruples as being too near of kin, and was on terms of intimate friendship with Desiderius, the abbot of Monte Cassino. A desire to deliver the Christians from the yoke of the Saracens was at least one of the motives which impelled Robert and his brother Roger to undertake the conquest of Sicily (1061). The gift of a banner blessed by the pope stimulated their ardour, and stamped the enterprise with a religious character. The Normans, in fact, won Southern Italy and Sicily for the Church of Rome. With the fall of Otranto (1068) and Bari (1071) the last foothold of the eastern emperors upon Italian soil was wrested from them; and by the conquest of Sicily, the wave of Mohammedan aggression was beaten back. The expulsion of the heretic and the infidel from that part of Europe was the work of the Normans, and opened a clear field there for the introduction of the papal sway.

ii. In South Italy

The good service which the Normans were doing for the Papacy in Italy and Sicily may have partly determined Hildebrand to support the great design of William of Normandy against England. We know, at any rate, that William's envoy, Gilbert of Lisieux, came to advocate the duke's claim to the English crown at the papal court a year after the consecrated banner had been sent to Roger in Sicily (1064).

iii. In England

[1] See above, p. 35.

There was no ambassador to plead the cause of England's liberties and England's king; but from Hildebrand's own pen (Epist. vii. 23), we learn that the question was earnestly debated amongst the cardinals, and that he was reproached by some of his colleagues for espousing William's side, and furthering a design which must lead to bloodshed. His counsels, however, prevailed, and the Norman conqueror of England, like the Norman conqueror of Sicily, led his army to victory beneath a banner blessed by the Roman pontiff. The sanction given to William's enterprise by the Pope may indeed be regarded as one of the masterstrokes of Hildebrand's genius. No heresy, no lack of respect for the Roman See, could fairly be laid to the charge of the English Church; she could boast of her saints and of her minsters as well as any Church in Christendom; but the insular position of the country was reflected in the character of the Church: in certain peculiarities of ritual and in the use of the vernacular, in its close connexion with the State, in its slowness, if not reluctance, to adopt some of the latest monastic reforms, and the decrees respecting clerical marriage, it was an intensely national Church. Hildebrand had the sagacity to see that if the enterprise of William succeeded, England would be brought within the more direct influence of Rome; for it would be closely connected with the Continent, it would be ruled by a man who was the friend of Lanfranc, the most learned champion of Roman doctrine and Roman rights, and would be occupied by a people whose countrymen were already in alliance with the Apostolic See. Thus the ecclesiastical even more than the political liberties of

England were overthrown on the day when William conquered Harold. As the appeal of William to the papal court strengthened the claim of the pope to dispose of crowns and kingdoms at his pleasure, so the conquest of England, sanctioned by the pope, seemed to give him a peculiar right over the English Church, and strengthened his pretension to be the supreme ruler of the Church in all other countries.

In Gaul, mainly through the influence of the Clugniacs, the Papacy found most zealous supporters. Even the fierce Fulk, count of Anjou, was a warm advocate of the reforms which the Hildebrandine party were pressing on the Church. During the minority of Philip I. the Church was almost the only restraining influence upon the prevailing lawlessness and disorder, partly through the institution of the 'Truce of God,' which required a cessation of hostilities during certain holy seasons—partly through the encouragement given by the pope to the nobles to turn their arms against the Saracens.

iv. Gaul

One of the most attractive fields of enterprise for military champions of the Church was Spain. After the Ommiad dynasty came to an end (1031) the dominion of the Arabs began to fall to pieces. The country was divided amongst a number of independent and rival emirs. The Christian population, had it been united, might easily have overcome them; but it lacked a central power. Sancho the Great, king of Castille and Navarre (1030) seemed likely to become such a leader, but he died in 1035, and his kingdom was partitioned between his sons. The stronger of these, Ferdinand I., was a vigorous

v. Spain

assailant of the Arabs, a friend of the Church, and a patron of the Clugniacs, but he would not render unqualified obedience to Rome, and received the censure of Leo IX. for supporting the archbishop of Compostella in his pretensions to the title of Apostolic Primate.[1] His nephew, Sancho Ramirez, defeated the Arabs in Aragon (1065), with the aid of William, duke of Aquitaine; and married a sister of count Ebulo of Rouci near Reims. These connexions with France opened the way for Rome into that part of Spain. In the neighbouring march of Barcelona the count Raymond-Berenger I. invited a legate from Rome. Cardinal Hugh was sent, who set to work with great vigour and success to establish the Roman Liturgy and Ordinal in the place of the old Visigothic Use, to enforce the decrees against simony and clerical marriage, and to introduce the custom of the 'Truce of God.' The mind of Hildebrand was much occupied with schemes for uniting French and Spanish nobles in a grand effort to expel the Arabs from Spain, to hold the conquered lands as vassals of the pope, and subjugate the Spanish Church completely to the Apostolic See.

Crossing to the other side of Europe, on the eastern borders of Germany, we find that Rome had lost some of the influence which she once had there in the days of St. Stephen, king of Hungary, and Boleslaw I., duke of Poland (1000-1030). The newly converted Slavs and Magyars had been some of the most devoted sons of the Church; but now, although Christianity survived, the organisation of the Church was in abeyance; the decrees against simony were not

vi. Hungary

[1] See above, p. 30.

enforced, the 'Truce of God' was not observed, there were no Clugniac houses to leaven the minds of the people, and papal legates were rarely sent. Nevertheless, here also the vigilant eye of Hildebrand watched for an opportunity of re-establishing papal authority. He maintained that Solomon, king of Hungary, had no right to acknowledge the German king as suzerain, that St. Stephen had held his crown direct from the pope Sylvester II., and that Henry III. had recognised the paramount right of Rome over the kingdom by sending a spear and crown to the pope after his victory over the Hungarian king. And in the strife between Solomon and his cousin Geisa which distracted the country some years later, Hildebrand saw a divine judgment for the defection of the king from his obedience to Rome.

vii. Poland
In Poland, duke Boleslaw was opposed to the suzerainty of the German king, but the downfall of the Church was so complete in that country, and the duke himself was so irreligious a man, that it was impossible for Rome to enter into a close alliance with him. In 1075, however, Hildebrand wrote a friendly letter to him, and sent legates to fix upon a place for the Metropolitan See.

With the duke of Bohemia, on the other hand, the relations of the popes had long been amicable. Nicolas

viii. Bohemia
II., in 1060, conferred upon duke Spitihnew the privilege of wearing a mitre, which was confirmed to his successor Wratislaw by Alexander II., and both dukes on receiving the honour paid 100 pounds of silver to Rome. The direct influence, however, of Rome on Bohemian affairs was small until a quarrel between Wratislaw and his brother Jerome

opened an opportunity for interference. Jerome, a young man of secular habits and adventurous spirit, had been forced into holy orders against his will, but he was covetous of the rich bishopric of Prague, which fell vacant in 1066. Wratislaw wished to bestow it on one of his own chaplains, but Jerome was so popular with the citizens of Prague that his brother dared not withhold it from him. He was consecrated by Siegfried of Mainz, and received investiture from king Henry. But open strife soon broke out between the brothers. Wratislaw had made Olmütz an episcopal see, to the great damage of the revenues of Prague. Jerome attacked the town with an armed force and captured the bishop, who was shamefully ill treated by his troops. Then Wratislaw complained to Rome (1072), a legate was sent who held a large synod of clergy and nobles, and suspended Jerome from his office. Jerome fled for protection to Siegfried of Mainz; but Siegfried, although jealous of the intrusion of Rome into the affairs of his province, dared not support him in the face of the threats and warnings which he received from the papal court. Jeromy then went to Rome and threw himself upon the mercy of the pope. His suspension was removed, but henceforth the pope took care that, in his diocese at least, the decrees against simony and the marriage of priests should be enforced. In Denmark, the king Swegen Estrithson had become religious in his old age, and paid obsequious deference to the authority of Rome. Partly through him, and partly through Adalbert of Bremen, pope Alexander could assert his sway over the Scandinavian Church.

ix. Scandinavia

Thus, all parts of Western Europe were being

gradually drawn more and more within the papal grasp. But the relations of the pope with Germany were in a peculiar and transitional stage. The power of the crown had been undermined by the encroachments of the nobles, especially during the minority of Henry IV. He himself had been brought up in a school of obedience to the Papacy; at the bidding of Rome he had abandoned the divorce from his wife, he had restored the property which his counsellors had taken from the Church during his minority, he had seen some of his earliest appointments to bishoprics cancelled by the pope, on divers pretexts, without offering any opposition. But at last he would give way no more. He and his counsellors perceived that his power in Lombardy was bound up with his right of investiture, and he resolved to uphold the nomination of Godfrey to the see of Milan at all costs. Early in the year 1073, he sent an envoy, Rapoto of Bohburg, across the Alps to enforce his will. Rapoto held a synod of Lombard bishops at Novara, declared the purpose of the king, and compelled them to consecrate Godfrey.

Here, then, was a direct collision between the authority of the king and the pope, who had excommunicated Godfrey, and declared Atto to be lawfully elected. At the Lenten synod in Rome, five of the king's counsellors, supposed to be responsible for his bold action, were excommunicated. But this strong measure did not produce submission, for the counsellors were not dismissed.

Henry had proved less pliant than was expected; nor could the pope rely upon very staunch support from the Church in Germany. For that Church maintained an attitude of considerable independence, the heritage, partly, of past days, when German sovereigns had made and unmade popes, and had been the chief rulers in ecclesiastical as well as secular affairs. The royal right of investiture was a close tie between the higher clergy and the throne; and none of them dreamed of disputing it. The spirit of reform had not made much way; Roman legates were rarely seen in Germany; simony and clerical marriage prevailed; the rule of Clugny had not been commonly adopted, except in Lotharingia; amongst the laity the 'Truce of God' was ill observed, and religious duties little regarded.

Nevertheless, in Germany, as elsewhere, the influence of Rome was gaining ground. The rule of Clugny, introduced by archbishop Anno in the monastery which he founded at Siegburg, gradually made its way into other houses. Hirschau, founded in 1069, became a kind of central house of the Clugniac order, from which men went forth who preached the Hildebrandine doctrines of reform in all parts of the country. One by one the greatest prelates in Germany were made to bow beneath the yoke of papal authority. Anno of Cöln, Siegfried of Mainz, Herman of Bamberg, Charles of Constanz—all had their day of humiliation before the Roman tribunal, and found that the strength of their position at home lay in obedience to the Apostolic See.

Above all, in the great struggle which was impending, the Roman pontiff could rely upon the majesty of his name and the august position which he now occupied in the eyes of Western Christendom. The Easter synods, which were now held annually at Rome, were legislative assemblies for the whole Church. They took the place, in some sort, of the imperial councils which had been held in the days of Charles the Great. The secular head of the empire had presided in those councils, which had dealt with ecclesiastical as well as civil affairs; the spiritual head presided in the Roman synods, which often issued decrees touching political almost as nearly as spiritual questions.

Peter Damiani regarded this tendency to interfere in secular matters with considerable misgiving and dis-
<small>Death of Peter Damiani</small> like; he protested against it, as he had against the military undertakings of Leo IX. But whatever check he may have exercised on the policy of Hildebrand was removed by his death, which occurred February 23, 1072.

On April 21, 1073, pope Alexander also died; and at
<small>and of pope Alexander II.</small> last the time was come when he who for twenty-five years had been the guiding mind of eight pontiffs should himself be called to occupy the papal chair.

CHAPTER IX.

HILDEBRAND ELECTED POPE. FIRST TWO YEARS OF HIS PONTIFICATE. 1073–75.

THE death of a pope was commonly the signal for a tumult in Rome, but on this occasion the city was
<small>Election of Hildebrand, April 22</small> tranquil. Hildebrand proclaimed a three days' fast and prayer, after which the cardinals were to proceed to election. But when the obsequies of the late pope were being performed in the Lateran Church the day after his death, a mixed multitude poured

into the church and a shout arose, 'Let Hildebrand be bishop!' Hildebrand strove to mount one of the 'ambons,' or reading-desks, in order to calm the tumult, but the cardinal Hugh thrust himself forward and addressed the assembly. 'Brethren,' he said, 'ye know how since the days of Leo IX. Hildebrand hath exalted the holy Roman Church and delivered our city from bondage. As it is impossible to find a better man, or, indeed, his equal, we elect him who has been ordained in our Church, and is well known and thoroughly approved amongst us.' The remonstrances of Hildebrand were drowned in a unanimous shout from cardinals, clergy, and people, 'St. Peter wills Hildebrand to be Pope.' Then, according to Hildebrand's own narrative, the people rushed upon him in a kind of frenzy, and dragged him to the Church of St. Pietro in Vincoli, where he was elected by the cardinals and other Roman clergy, with the consent of bishops and abbots, clergy and monks, and the approval of the people expressed by acclamation. He was declared to be elected as 'a man eminent in piety and learning, a lover of equity and justice, firm in adversity, temperate in prosperity, according to the Apostolic precept (1 Tim. iii. 2), " of good behaviour, modest, sober, chaste, hospitable, ruling his house well," brought up and taught from boyhood within the bosom of this our Church, already for his merits advanced to the office of archdeacon, whom now and henceforth we will to be called Gregory, Pope and Apostolic Primate.'

Exhausted with agitation, Gregory spent a few days in retirement, writing letters to his friends, Desiderius, abbot of Monte Cassino; Gisulf, count of Salerno;

Wibert, archbishop of Ravenna; the countesses Beatrice and Matilda; Swegen Estrithson, king of Denmark; Manasse, archbishop of Reims; Hugh, abbot of Clugny; and others, announcing his election and begging their prayers, sympathy, and support in the arduous and perilous office to which he had most unwillingly been called.

One question of vital importance touching the election of Hildebrand was never positively settled. The right of Henry to have some voice in the election of a pope was vaguely, indeed, yet expressly, reserved by the decree of Nicolas II.,[1] but the king did not at this time claim the right, nor try to get it more clearly defined. If he never distinctly confirmed the election of Hildebrand, neither did he oppose it: he acquiesced in it, and Gregory, on his part, did not seek or ask for the royal assent.

The tone which he intended to adopt towards the king is clearly indicated in a letter (dated May 6, 1073) addressed to duke Godfrey. He declares that no one could be more anxious than he was for the king's welfare, temporal and eternal; he purposed, therefore, to send messengers on the first opportunity to convey his paternal love and admonition touching such things as, in his judgment, concerned the advancement of the Church and the honour of the king. If he hearkened to his counsels it would be to his great profit, and to the Pope's great joy; 'but if,' continued Gregory, 'he returns hatred for love, and treats the divine honour bestowed on him with contempt, we will not, God helping us, incur the curse

Letter of Hildebrand to duke Godfrey

[1] See above, p. 47.

pronounced on him "who keepeth back his sword from blood" (Jerem. xlviii. 10). For we are not at liberty to prefer the favour of any man to the law of God, or to swerve from the straight path for the sake of advantage, as saith the Apostle, "If I sought to please men I should not be the servant of God."'

It is clear that if Gregory wished to act the part of a father to Henry he intended to exact absolute obedience from his son. Language nearly identical is used in a letter written about a month later (June 24) to Beatrice and Matilda, in which he also warns them against holding any communication with Godfrey, the simoniacal archbishop of Milan, or with the bishops who had consecrated him.

Henry had been urged by some of the bishops in Lombardy and Germany to pronounce the election of Gregory invalid, because the royal assent had not been asked; but Henry was threatened with a revolt in Saxony, and did not care to embroil himself in additional troubles in Italy. On May 22 Gregory was ordained priest, and on June 29 he was consecrated without any opposition; indeed, the presence at the ceremony of Gregory, bishop of Vercelli, the king's chancellor, might perhaps be regarded as a token of the royal assent.

Gregory consecrated June 29, 1073

The name of Gregory was already renowned throughout Western Europe; all countries had felt the force of his will, and a thrill of hope or fear must have vibrated in every part of Christendom when it was known that he was now supreme pontiff. Much, however, as had been accomplished (and mainly through his energy) since the reformation of the papacy began, he declared (in his letter to duke Godfrey) that he was overwhelmed by the prospect of the task which lay before him; he would rather have died and been at rest in Christ than live on in the midst of such perils; nothing but trust in God and the prayers of good men could save him from sinking beneath the load of anxiety; for the whole world was lying in wickedness; all men, and especially they who held high office in the Church, in their thirst for gain and the glory of this world, were disturbers rather than defenders of the Church, the enemies rather than the friends of religion and justice.

But whatever Gregory's inward fears and anxieties might be, there was no outward sign of his flinching from the work which lay before him; he brought to his task all the zeal of a monk and the ability of a statesman. His first and chief aim was, of course, to strengthen his position in Italy. To protect the patrimony of St. Peter he formed a kind of local militia in which many of the Roman nobility were enrolled, and garrisons were placed in the towns and border castles. Towards the Church in Lombardy he immediately assumed a dignified and commanding attitude, and prelates and people were charged on their allegiance to the Roman Church, 'the mistress, as they know, of all Christendom,' to abstain from all intercourse with the impious, simoniacal, excommunicated Godfrey.

One matter of primary importance was to put his relations with the Normans on a satisfactory footing. His visit to South Italy Robert Wiscard fell ill in the spring of 1073, and there was a report that he was dead. Gregory sent envoys to Bari to offer condolence to the widow, and demand fealty from her son Roger, but when they reached Bari they found that the report was false. Robert had recovered, and politely informed the envoys that the pope might rely upon him as a trusty vassal. Gregory, however, was not satisfied with specious but vague promises. In the summer he made a progress into South Italy, and summoned Robert to do homage at St. Germano. But Robert came not; he was suspicious of the pope's friendship with his rivals Richard of Capua, Landulf of Benevento, and Gisulf of Salerno. Gregory withdrew to Benevento, and desired Robert to meet him and pay him homage there. The Norman leader so far obeyed as to appear outside the town, but he was accompanied by a large band of armed followers; he refused to enter the town, and Gregory declined to visit him in his camp, whereupon he and his men departed, to the annoyance, but perhaps also partly to the relief, of the pope.

The suspicious attitude of Robert made Gregory all the more anxious to bind the other chiefs in South Italy more closely to the apostolic see. Treaties were made with Landulf of Benevento, and Richard of Capua, by which they pledged themselves to defend the person of the pope, and the property of the Holy See, and never to invest anyone with a church benefice without the papal sanction. Richard undertook to pay a yearly tribute to Rome, and to put all churches in his territory under the direct jurisdiction of the pope. Even obedience to the temporal head of the empire is made conditional on the will of the spiritual head, and . secondary to allegiance to him. 'To king Henry I will swear fealty whensoever I may be admonished thereto by thee or thy successors, and saving always my fealty to the Holy Roman Church.'

Gregory was indeed at this time sanguine of obtaining complete mastery over the king. In a letter to Rudolf of Swabia (September 1, 1073) he thanks the duke effusively for labouring to bring about a good understanding between himself and Henry. To further this end and arrange the terms of a lasting peace he invites Rudolf to meet the empress Agnes, the countess Beatrice, the bishop of Como, and others at Rome. He observes that the welfare of the Empire and of the Church depended on harmony between the chief sacerdotal and secular powers, which were to the whole body of the faithful as the two eyes to the human body; and he was under a personal obligation to be Henry's friend, having been treated with peculiar kindness by his father, who had also with his dying breath commended his son to the care of the Roman Church. Gregory's hopes were raised still higher by receiving before the end of the month (September) a letter from Henry himself, confessing and bewailing his sins, promising amendment, and professing submission to the Roman See in language so meek and contrite that Gregory admits the like had never been addressed before to any pope by any king. The tone of the letter is indeed so abject that no one who knew the passionate, headstrong nature of the king could have supposed that he would abide by it for long. It was written, as we shall presently see, when he was encompassed with danger, and it was probably dictated to him by some one whom he dared not resist.

There were indeed strong political reasons just then

why the king and the pope should wish to be on good terms; each wanted the support of the other. Rebellion had broken out in Saxony. In Italy the league between the papacy and the lords of Capua and Benevento provoked the jealousy of Robert Wiscard. He summoned his brother Roger from Sicily, and invaded the territory of Capua. Gregory, who had been sojourning there three months, retreated towards Rome about the end of November. Richard kept his hold on Capua, but Robert and Roger ravaged his lands, and then, moving on towards Benevento, they treated that territory in like manner. At the Christmas synod, therefore, in Rome (1074) Gregory solemnly excommunicated Robert, for his sacrilegious attack on the property of the Holy See.

Robert Wiscard's aggressions

He is excommunicated by Gregory

Soon after this an embassy was sent to Germany consisting of the cardinal-bishops Hubert of Palestrina and Gerald of Ostia, as legates, accompanied by the bishops of Como and Chur, and the empress Agnes. The king was keeping Easter at Bamberg, but the legates would not meet him there, because Herman, the bishop, was notoriously simoniacal. They were received with due honours at Nürnberg, where the king formally renewed his profession of repentance and submission in their presence, and his counsellors having taken an oath to restore all Church property obtained through simony were released from excommunication. The legates then demanded the summons of a national council, in which they would preside and proclaim the decrees of the last synod at Rome against simony and clerical marriage. But the German bishops objected to Roman legates presiding in

Papal embassy to Germany

a national council. If the pope did not preside in person, the office of president, they said, belonged to the archbishop of Mainz. The legates stormed and cited the archbishops of Mainz and Bremen, the chief instigators of opposition, to answer for their conduct at Rome. They were obliged to leave, however, without holding the council; but they returned home laden with gifts, and bearing a friendly letter from Henry to the pope. Gregory attributed his submissive behaviour to the influence of his mother, and wrote a grateful letter to her, expressing the liveliest hope of a lasting reconciliation with the king. To the archbishops Siegfried of Mainz and Liemar of Bremen he wrote letters of sharp reproof, peremptorily citing them to appear at the next Lenten synod in Rome, and suspending Liemar from his functions during the interval. To Henry, in December, he wrote a very kindly letter, thanking him for his reception of the legates, expressing his joy at hearing that he intended to put down simony and clerical concubinage, and proposing that the dispute about the see of Milan should be settled by a conference.

But the project which most absorbed the mind of Gregory during the year 1074 was an expedition to the East. The emperor Michael VII. wrote a letter to Gregory in 1073, craving the help of Western Christendom against the Seljuk Turks, and suggesting hopes of a reunion between the Eastern and Western branches of the Church. Gregory responded to the appeal with alacrity; he sent the patriarch of Venice to Constantinople as his envoy, he wrote to the counts William of Burgundy, Raymond of St. Gilles, and Amadeus of Savoy (February, 1074),

Gregory's projected expedition to the East

urging them to muster forces for the defence of the East from the infidel, and in March he addressed a circular letter to all the faithful, especially beyond the Alps, to come to the rescue of their Eastern brethren. But his grand project broke down. In April he wrote to Godfrey of Lotharingia, upbraiding him for not sending the soldiers which he had promised; in June he left Rome and went to a spot near Viterbo, where the Tuscan troops were to assemble, but the Pisans refused to serve under Gisulf of Salerno, whom he had appointed commander, and Beatrice and Matilda, who had promised in their zeal to raise 30,000 men, were hindered from fulfilling their promise by an insurrection amongst their vassals. The disappointment was all the more bitter to him because he had reckoned upon using his crusading army to overawe Robert Wiscard—the one power in Italy which was really formidable to him. Robert had been summoned to Benevento, where Gregory had hoped to display his host of crusaders before him, and then release him from the ban of the Church if he seemed submissive. But things turned out the other way: Robert came indeed to Benevento, but with a strong army of vassals; and the pope, who had none, dared not meet him. Worry and vexation brought on a severe illness, in which his life was almost despaired of. By October he had recovered, but wrote in a most desponding strain to Beatrice and Matilda about the failure of his plans and the general corruption of faith and morals in Christendom. His recovery from sickness caused him sorrow, he said, rather than joy, and his whole soul was yearning for that better country where the weary would be at rest.

Two months later, however, his hopes had revived. He writes to the king (December 7) telling him that he has more than 50,000 men ready to march, under his own guidance, to the East, against the enemies of God. He begs Henry to give him counsel and aid, and commends the chief care of the Church to him in his absence. He himself would rather die for the deliverance of the faithful than be the ruler of the whole world; above all things, he longed to reclaim the Eastern Church from error and lead it back in obedience to the Apostolic See. He proposed that the countess Matilda and the empress Agnes should accompany him as pilgrims on this pious expedition. With such sisters by his side he would gladly lay down his life for Christ, assured of meeting them again in the everlasting home.

But these bright visions of glory speedily dissolved; the project was everywhere received with cold indifference or positive opposition. At last the emperor made overtures to Robert Wiscard, accompanied by handsome gifts; the daughter of Robert was betrothed to the son of the emperor, and the heir of the Cæsars obtained from a Norman adventurer the aid which he had sought in vain from the supreme pontiff of the West. It was a mortifying blow to the ambition of Gregory; on January 22, 1075, he wrote in deep dejection to Hugh, abbot of Clugny; he implores his friend to pray, as he did himself, that the Lord would either come to the rescue of His suffering Church, or release His servant from this world of misery and load of care. 'Turn to what quarter of the world he would, he found scarce any bishops who ruled their flocks from the pure love of Christ rather than from worldly ambition, and among princes there were none who preferred the honour of God and His righteousness to their own gain. And as for the Romans, Lombards, and Normans among whom he dwelt, they were worse, as he often told them to their face, than Jews and Pagans.

He had, some months earlier, written a letter to Manasse, archbishop of Reims, in which he drew a frightful picture of the disorders and moral corruption of the kingdom of France, accused the king, Philip I., of being the chief instigator of rapine and every species of wickedness, and upbraided the bishops with being dumb dogs, who did nothing to protect their Church and country from spoliation and ruin. Unless they compelled the king to desist from his simoniacal appointments and his deeds of violence and oppression, he would lay his kingdom under interdict, and by God's help pluck him down from the throne which he disgraced; and unless the bishops did their duty more zealously, he would deprive them of their office. This tone of excessive severity, and the haughtiness of the legates whom he sent to France, roused a spirit of resistance amongst the French clergy with which even the Clugniacs had some sympathy. But in Lombardy and Germany the disaffection was more deeply seated. The decrees against simony and clerical marriage were little regarded; the peremptory citations to the German bishops to attend the Lent synod at Rome were met with polite evasions or blunt refusals.

Resistance to papal authority in France and Germany

The Lent synod sat from February 24 to 28, and Gregory was not sparing in his use of spiritual weapons. Five counsellors of king Henry were excommunicated for simony. The suspension of archbishop Liemar was renewed, and the same punishment was inflicted on Bishop Werner of Strasburg and Henry of Speier. Herman of Bamberg was threatened with it, unless he came to Rome before Easter and cleared his character before the Pope. In Lombardy, the bishops of Pavia and Turin were suspended, the bishop of Piacenza deposed. Excommunication was again pronounced on Robert Wiscard, and Philip, king of France, was warned that the same fate would befall him unless he gave some assurances of amendment to the papal legates.

Synod in Rome, 1075

Four decrees against simony and clerical marriage were promulgated at this synod: (i.) all priests who had purchased their orders or office were forbidden to minister again in the Church; (ii.) any benefice obtained by money was to be forfeited; (iii.) priests convicted of incontinence were to be degraded; (iv.) the laity were to reject the ministrations of any priests who disobeyed these injunctions. But the most momentous decree was that which declared investiture by laymen with any ecclesiastical office absolutely uncanonical. The reforming party had for some time past been opposed to the custom of laymen bestowing the symbolical ring and staff upon bishops or abbots; but now, for the first time, it was condemned by an authoritative judgment from the Apostolic chair. Such a decree obviously touched the royal power in Germany and Italy in its tenderest point. It looks as if Gregory was now determined to leave the king no choice between absolute submission and an open rupture with Rome. Henry had not as yet fulfilled his own promises, or hearkened to the demands of Gregory. He had done nothing to settle the disputed succession

at Milan, or to put down simony and clerical marriage;
he had not compelled the German bishops to attend the
Lent synod at Rome, which Gregory in his letter of
December (1074) had requested him to do. Gregory,
however, invited him to send some discreet counsellors
to Rome, to confer on the possibility of softening the
canon about investiture. Certainly this canon was not
so publicly circulated as the others; it was not, like
them, inserted in all letters written to bishops about
this time, and several years later many of the German
bishops could profess themselves ignorant of it. In
fact, it seems to have been suspended as a kind of threat
over Henry's head, in the hope of inducing him to come
to terms—only terms with Gregory meant nothing short
of absolute surrender. He intended to keep the king
rigorously to the language of humble submission employed in his letter two years before. At present he
may have hoped to get the support of the king in reducing the clergy to obedience; but in their subjugation Henry might dread his own, and he soon showed
that he had no mind to abide slavishly by words which
had been wrung from him in an hour of need and almost
of despair.

CHAPTER X.

REVOLT OF THE SAXONS. BEGINNINGS OF STRIFE BETWEEN HENRY IV. AND THE POPE. 1073–76.

EVER since Henry began to reign Saxony had been a
source of anxiety. The people were hardy and fierce;
they thought that they had been harshly treated by

REVOLT OF THE SAXONS 103

Henry III., and they were soon profoundly discontented with the rule of his son. Henry had built castles to overawe them, but the cruelty and licentiousness of the soldiers who occupied them only exasperated the native peasantry to fury, while the Saxon nobles were extremely jealous of the king's partiality for Swabians, and indignant at his holding the duchy of Saxony in his own hands, and keeping Magnus, the heir of the late duke Ordulf, in confinement. Rightly or wrongly they imagined that an expedition, announced by Henry to be undertaken, in the summer of 1073, against the Poles, would be turned against Saxony, and that the whole country would be enslaved and handed over to the occupation of Swabians. Nobles and prelates discussed their wrongs in secret cabals; the archbishop of Magdeburg, the bishops of Halberstadt and Hildersheim, Otto, the deposed duke of Bavaria, and the margrave Dedi were the chief leaders of sedition; but the archbishops of Bremen and the bishops of Osnabrück and Zeitz adhered to the king. On the very day on which Hildebrand was being consecrated pope (June 29) the malcontents held a conference, at the close of which they sent messengers to the king at Goslar, informing him that they could not join the expedition to Poland, demanding the demolition of the Saxon castles, the restitution of lands which he had violently seized, the dismissal of his evil counsellors who were ruining him and his kingdom, the removal of the concubines by whom his court was defiled, and the restoration of his wife to her proper position. If he did these things they would serve him faithfully; but if not they would fight to the last gasp for the Church, for the faith, and for their own freedom and honour. The

Insurrection in Saxony

king consulted with his friends, who recommended a harsh reply, not unlike that suggested by the evil counsellors of Rehoboam.

On August 9 Henry threw himself into the strong castle of the Harzburg; the Saxon insurgents closely blockaded it, but the king escaped by night, and after four days' hard travelling through the forest southwards, arrived, almost famished, at the monastery of Hersfeld. Here his friends rallied round him, including some of the nobles who had been summoned to the expedition against Poland. Henry fell at their feet and passionately entreated them to be faithful to him; many were moved to tears, and pledged themselves to stand by him, but for a time no definite plan of action was devised. The king remained at Hersfeld, and, during his sojourn there, despatched the penitent and submissive letter to the Pope to which reference has been already made.[1]

Flight of Henry from the Harzburg

The Saxons meanwhile, aided by the Thuringians, laid vigorous siege to the king's castles, and by the end of August many of them were taken.

The king was alarmed and anxious to make terms; Siegfried of Mainz, at his request, met the insurgent leaders at Corbey, and arranged that a conference should be held at Gerstungen on October 20, on condition that the Saxons abstained in the interval from attacking the castles. On the day appointed the Saxon leaders came with 14,000 armed followers; the king was represented by the archbishops of Mainz and Cöln, the bishops of Metz and Bamberg, the dukes Rudolf of Swabia and Berthold of Carinthia.

First conference at Gerstungen

[1] See above, pp. 95, 102.

Henry himself awaited the issue at Wurzburg. The Saxons recounted their tale of wrongs, dwelling especially upon the gross licentiousness of the king's habits when he resided in their country. The assembly heard their statements with horror, and after three days' deliberation it was resolved to depose the king and make a new election, but the choice was to be left to a larger assembly to be held at Christmas, and the resolution was not publicly announced.

Henry moved to Regensberg, where he spent All Saints' day, and thence to Nürnberg. Whilst he was there strange tales were circulated by a man named Reginger, that he had been bribed by the king to assassinate the dukes Rudolf and Berthold, and although Henry indignantly denied the charge, offering to prove his innocence in single combat, the nobles became suspicious and held aloof from court. The situation of the king became pitiably forlorn; he fell very ill, and his enemies began to hope that his death would end their troubles; but early in December he recovered and visited Worms, where he was warmly welcomed by the people; and, on the other hand, an attempt made by the archbishop of Mainz to convene a council for the election of a new king was a total failure.

Christmas was spent at Worms, but without any splendour, for Henry had but little money and few companions. Gregory meanwhile wrote a letter (December 20) to the archbishop of Magdeburg and the other leaders of the revolt, declaring his will that both sides should lay down their arms until the arrival of his legate, who would investigate the causes of strife.

Henry, however, had resolved, probably before the Pope wrote, to try and relieve his besieged garrisons in Saxony. He mustered a force with difficulty, and in January, 1074, set out from Worms. The cold was intense, and the sufferings of his army were terrible. No battle took place; but nearly two months were consumed in conferences with the insurgents, who adhered firmly to their old conditions—the destruction of the castles, the reformation of the king's conduct, and respect for the rights and liberties of his people. For some time Henry strove to parry their proposals, but at last he gave way and accepted their terms. Even then he was so tardy in action that the Saxons surrounded the palace at Goslar with an armed force, and threatened him with deposition if he did not keep his word. The archbishop of Bremen and other friends besought him to yield, and at last he issued his orders for the demolition of the castles.

He retired to Worms in an irritable frame of mind, and irritation was presently inflamed to rage by the tidings that, three days after his departure from Saxony, a mob of peasants had burnt the great church which he had built near the Harzburg, ransacked the tombs of his son and brother, upset the altars, and disturbed the reliques of the saints which lay beneath. The Saxon nobles sent messengers to the king, solemnly asserting their innocence of these outrages; but they could not pacify his fury. Since human force and law did not avail him in the contest, he would now send to Rome and invoke divine assistance against his sacrilegious enemies. The papal legates who had been despatched

Insurgents burn the church at the Harzburg, 1074

from Rome in March met the king, as we have seen,[1] at Nürnberg about Easter, and his submissive demeanour to them would be quite accounted for by his anxiety to secure the aid of the pope in his struggle with the Saxons. How Henry's cause was represented by them at Rome, or by his own messengers whom he is said to have sent, we do not know, but Gregory did not excommunicate the Saxons, as the king had hoped. On the other hand, the sympathy of the nobles began to revert to Henry after the outrage at Goslar; many returned to court, declared themselves ready to help him in punishing the Saxons, and were taken back into favour.

The summer of 1074 was mainly occupied by an abortive expedition into Hungary, to aid Henry's brother-in-law, king Solomon, against an attack made by his own cousins in conjunction with the Poles. The country was laid so utterly waste by the enemy that Henry could not get supplies for his army, and was forced to retreat.

He spent Christmas at Strasburg, where he gradually got together a large army, with which he set out for Saxony, in the spring of 1075. In June the Saxons were totally defeated in a great battle by the river Unstrut in Thuringia, though the king's side also suffered heavy loss. Henry tried to give the war a religious complexion. Siegfried of Mainz pronounced the enemy excommunicate, and affected to have a commission from the pope, but when or how obtained it would be hard to say. In July the army was disbanded for want of supplies, but reassembled again at Gerstungen in October. On the 22nd a conference was

[1] See above, p. 96.

opened here between the Saxon leaders and some representatives of the king, foremost amongst whom <small>The peace of</small> was Godfrey of Lotharingia. Godfrey was <small>Gerstungen</small> hunchbacked and little of stature, but he far surpassed all the other nobles in wisdom and eloquence, as well as in the abundance of his wealth and the excellence of his troops. He was the pivot upon which everything turned, and his influence at length induced the Saxons to surrender. On October 26, 1075, Henry received their formal unqualified submission. The principal leaders were handed over to the custody of his friends, and their lands allotted to his followers who had distinguished themselves in the war. The Harzburg and other castles were rebuilt, and Saxony soon wore the aspect of a conquered province.

Up to this time Gregory had seemed to hope, perhaps had really hoped, to subject Henry's will to his own, <small>Beginning of dissension between the pope and the king</small> and as long as Germany was unsettled and Saxony unsubdued, there was a fair prospect of succeeding in this aim. But the defeat of the Saxons strengthened Henry's position and raised his reputation, and he soon began to manifest more independence of spirit. Up to July 1075, the letters of Gregory to the king are friendly; he is praised for making some efforts to check simony, and to enforce the celibacy of the clergy; and the pope's hopes were yet further raised by receiving a letter from him saying that he had sent some confidential messengers to Rome to confer with him about the questions at issue, unknown to the nobles, who seemed to wish to sow dissension between them. But the messengers, eagerly expected by Gregory, came not; on the way they were overtaken by an envoy from the king, bidding them halt at a certain distance from Rome. This envoy had been sent after the king's victory over the Saxons, and carried the news of it to Gregory, who sent back a letter by him to the king, congratulating him on his success, and warning him to use it wisely and well.

Soon after this, the pope heard, to his annoyance, that Henry had informed the countesses Beatrice and Matilda that he could not settle the disputed questions without the consent of the nobles. This was a departure from his former proposal to keep his communications with Gregory private; but it is easy to see how the change came about. As long as he was doubtful of the support of the nobles in his contest with Saxony, and of the issue, he was anxious to retain the favour of the pope; but the nobles had stood by him, his victory had been gained by their aid, and he now wished to keep on good terms with them. From this date Gregory regarded him with great suspicion.

The bishop of Bamberg had been deposed at Rome for gross simony, and for trying to propitiate the papal tribunal by rich bribes. Henry and archbishop Siegfried were requested by Gregory to name a fitting man to fill the vacancy, but in December the king put one of his own favourites, Rupert of Goslar, into the see; he openly practised investiture with the ring and staff, his excommunicated counsellors were retained at court, the decrees enjoining celibacy were insolently defied by the clergy throughout the kingdom. To enforce these, however, would certainly have been a hard task. From the first the German clergy had offered the most violent and stubborn opposition to them: they would rather, they said, abandon their orders than their wives, and then the pope might rule the Church through angels, if he could get them. Archbishop Siegfried had introduced to his synod at Mainz (October, 1075) the bishop of Chur, who was the bearer of papal letters and mandates on the subject; but such a fierce tumult arose that the prelates were glad to escape from the assembly with their lives.

Another cause of complaint against the king was the part which he took in the dispute concerning the archbishopric of Milan.

Milanese affairs

In the spring of the year 1075 another attempt of the Patarines to alter the Ambrosian Rite had provoked a fierce tumult, in which Erlembald, their leader, was killed. This event revived the hopes of the anti-reformers in all parts of Italy. Gregory had bitter enemies in Rome, where he had tried to put down the extortion and robbery which pilgrims suffered at the hands of avaricious priests. A citizen named Cencius,[1] and cardinal Hugh, a man of restless and disappointed ambition, became the leaders of opposition, and they allied themselves with Wibert, archbishop of Ravenna, and Gregory of Vercelli, the king's chancellor, who were at the head of the disaffected in Lombardy. In the autumn, after the defeat of the Saxons, count Eberhard appeared in Lombardy as the king's representative, held a large diet in the Roncaglian plain, praised the Milanese for their bold resistance to the Patarines, and recommended them to send a deputation to his master's court, asking him to nominate a new archbishop. He

[1] Not to be confounded with Cencius the Prefect, a warm friend of Gregory.

and Gregory even made overtures to Robert Wiscard, inviting him to enter into alliance with them, and hold his lands as a fief from the king. But Robert rejected their offer: he had won his lands, he said, from the Greeks and Saracens by his sword, with the help of God, and the blessed Peter and Paul, and his allegiance was due to the Holy See. The ambassadors returned laden with gifts, marvelling at the wealth and power of the Normans and the ability of their leader. About this time, however, Robert and Richard of Capua made a joint attack upon the march of Camerino and duchy of Spoleto, which was displeasing to Gregory and alarming to duke Godfrey and the king, for Godfrey held the territory under the king, while the popes had long claimed it as a possession of the Roman See. The Normans, as usual, defeated the Italian troops, and the inhabitants of the duchy had henceforth to pay them an annual tribute. It was no doubt with a view to strengthening his hold upon the country that Henry now bestowed the bishoprics of Spoleto and Fermo upon Germans. They were appointed without any consultation with the pope, but were sent to Rome for consecration. This was a grave offence; but a far greater one was the nomination by the king of a new archbishop at Milan. Henry selected Tedald, a Milanese of high birth, but long resident in Germany, as a royal chaplain. He was invested by the king, and conducted by his envoys to Milan, where he arrived in November, and was warmly welcomed.

Thus the papal power was shaken from one end of Italy to the other. Gregory saw there was no escape from direct strife with the king, and plunged boldly into it. On December 7 he wrote to Tedald, commanding him to attend the next Lent synod in Rome, and forbidding his consecration until his case should be decided there. On the 8th he wrote to Gregory of Vercelli and the other suffragans of Milan, forbidding them to consecrate Tedald under pain of excommunication. Tedald was bidden to remember that the might of kings and conquerors weighed but as dust and ashes against the power of God and His apostles; the prelates were warned that if they contended with their mother, the holy Roman Church, they would find it 'hard to kick against the pricks.'

On the same day he wrote to the king, the last letter he ever addressed to him. He begins by saying that he hesitates to greet him with an apostolic blessing so long as he persists in associating with men who are under the ban of the Church. The submissive tone of his letters was in strange contrast with his conduct, his uncanonical appointments to the sees of Milan, Spoleto, and Fermo, and his negligence in enforcing the decrees against simony and the marriage of priests. He should be mindful of his high position, and show his gratitude to God for the recent victory over his enemies by more zealous devotion to God's Church. The tone of the letter is one of serious yet not unfriendly warning, but the bearers of it were entrusted with an oral message which was far more severe. They were to tell the king that he deserved to be deposed as well as excommunicated on account of his immoral life, and that unless he amended his conduct, and parted from his evil counsellors, who were under the Church's ban. before the

<small>Last letter from Gregory to the king</small>

STRIFE BETWEEN HENRY IV. AND THE POPE 113

next Lent synod, he would certainly be visited with excommunication.

The pope's messengers reached the court at Goslar on January 1, 1076. Henry, still elated with his victory over the Saxons, was in no docile mood. The accusations of profligacy had been originally made by the Saxons, and the worst of them at any rate had never been proved. Yet the pope's language implied that he believed them all, and as he had already demanded the release of the Saxon bishops until he should have decided their cause, the king began to suspect him of sympathy with his foes. He submitted the message to his friends, who professed the deepest indignation. If the pope, they said, audaciously threatened him with deposition, it would be well that he should, like some of his forefathers, depose the pope. The German bishops were accordingly summoned to a council, to be held at Worms on January 24, to consider what line of action should be taken.

Meanwhile the prospect of strife between the king and the pope had emboldened Gregory's enemies to make an attempt upon his life. He was keeping the vigil of Christmas-day in the church of St. Maria Maggiore; the congregation was small, for the night was very dark and the rain fell in torrents. Suddenly an armed throng burst into the church and rushed into the choir, where Gregory was celebrating mass; one of the party aimed a blow with a sword at his head, which would have been fatal had not the man slipped and fallen as he dealt it. The pope's breast, however, was gashed, he

Attempt on the pope's life in Rome

was stripped of his robes, dragged out, and carried off on horseback behind one of the soldiers to a strong tower belonging to Cencius. Two faithful friends, a man of humble rank and a noble matron, followed him there; the man wrapped him in furs and warmed his feet in his own bosom, while the lady staunched and bound up his wound. Meanwhile the clergy had sounded an alarm in the city, and in the early morning the tower was besieged by an enraged multitude. Cencius, overwhelmed with fear, flung himself at the pope's feet and implored his mercy. Gregory had never lost his dignity and self-possession. 'Thy injuries to myself,' he said, 'I freely pardon; thy sin against the Lord, His Mother, His Apostles, His Church must be expiated. Go on a pilgrimage to Jerusalem, and if thou returnest alive surrender thyself to me that I may decide how thou mayest be reconciled to God. As thou hast been an example of *per*version, so henceforth be an example of *con*version.' The pope then appeared at a balcony and waved his hand to reassure the people, but they mistook the gesture for a signal of distress, and some of them clambering over the outer wall forced their way into the tower, brought him out and conducted him to the church, where he completed the service which had been so strangely interrupted on the preceding night. Cencius, with his wife, fled from Rome, but instead of going on a pilgrimage, he conspired with the pope's enemies in Lombardy to undermine his power. Cardinal Hugh also was untiring in his efforts to knit them all into one strong party. He hurried from Germany to visit Wibert of Ravenna, and assist in the consecration of archbishop Tedald, and then hastened back to attend the Council of Worms and poison the mind of the assembly against the pope.

CHAPTER XI.

THE COUNCIL OF WORMS. HENRY IV. UNDER THE BAN OF THE CHURCH. 1076-77.

THE council met at Worms on the appointed day, January 24, 1076. Twenty-four German bishops were present, one Burgundian and one Italian. Only two archbishops came: Siegfried of Mainz and Udo of Trier. Anno of Cöln had died the month before, and his successor, a creature of Henry's, was not yet consecrated. The archbishops of Bremen and Salzburg held aloof. There was a large gathering of abbots, but they took no important part in the proceedings. Siegfried presided. The most influential layman present was, of course, duke Godfrey. Cardinal Hugh brought forward incredible accusations against Gregory of licentiousness, cruelty, witchcraft, and of using bribery and violence to obtain the Papacy. Few could have believed such calumnies, but at this moment the sympathy of the council was with the king. He had just been victorious in war; the pope was unpopular with the German clergy, and had countenanced unproven charges against Henry's character. A resolution renouncing obedience to Gregory was signed by all the bishops, except Adalbert of Wurzburg and

Meeting of the council at Worms

Herman of Metz, and their scruples or fears were presently overcome by the vehemence of William, the aged bishop of Utrecht. The bishops then drew up a letter addressed to 'brother Hildebrand,' as they dared to call him, setting forth the reasons why they renounced their obedience: his despotic government, which had brought schism and confusion into the Church; the irregularity of his election, without the consent of the heir to the empire; his intimacy with the countesses Beatrice and Matilda, and their interference in ecclesiastical affairs, which was a scandal to the Church.

<small>Gregory deposed by the council</small>

A letter in the king's own name repeated all these charges, but in more insulting terms. 'Henry, king, not by usurpation, but by God's holy ordinance, to Hildebrand, not pope, but the false monk. How darest thou, who hast won thy power through craft, flattery, bribery, and force, stretch forth thine hand against the Lord's anointed, despising the precept of the true pope, St. Peter: "Fear God, honour the king"? Condemned by the voice of all our bishops, quit the apostolic chair, and let another take it, who will preach the sound doctrine of St. Peter, and not do violence under the cloak of religion. I, Henry, by the grace of God, king, with all my bishops, say unto thee, "Get thee down, get thee down!"'

It was resolved that the decree of the council should be laid before the bishops of Lombardy, and then publicly announced in Rome, and that the Romans should be invited to receive a new pope at the hands of the king. Huzman and Burchard, the bishops of Speier and Basel, with count Eberhard, started immediately for

Italy, and the resolution of the council was approved at a synod held in Piacenza.

Henry also wrote a private letter to the pope informing him that his arrogant treatment of the bishops in Germany had become intolerable, and that his iniquities, revealed at the Council of Worms, proved that he had forfeited his right to the Apostolic chair. By his authority, therefore, as Patrician, the king bade him descend from it. In another letter to the Roman people he charged them to insist upon Gregory's abdication, and to accept another pope whom he would appoint after counsel with them and the bishops.

It was not easy to find a messenger bold enough to deliver these terrific documents at Rome; but at last Roland, a priest of Parma, was induced, by the offer of a large reward, to undertake the errand.

<small>Announcement of the deposition in Rome</small>

The Lent synod was held on February 21 in the Lateran church. The empress Agnes was present, 110 bishops attended, all from Italy and Gaul, a large number of abbots and monks, and a promiscuous throng of Roman clergy and laity. The hymn 'Veni, Creator' had been sung, and the assembly was absorbed in the examination of a portent—an egg on which the form of a black snake seemed to be traceable, writhing beneath a shield pressed down upon its head—when Roland entered, and, addressing Gregory, cried aloud : 'The king and our bishops bid thee come down from the chair of Peter, which thou hast gained by robbery.' Then, turning to the cardinals, he said : 'Ye are bidden to receive another pope from the king, who will come hither at Pentecost; for this man is no pope, but a ravening wolf.' The assembly was convulsed with horror and rage. The cardinal-bishop of Porto shouted, ' Seize him ! ' and Cencius, the prefect, would have rushed upon the envoy and hewn him in pieces had not Gregory shielded him with his own person. The pope received the documents from Roland's hand, and bade him sit at his feet ; and then, with unruffled calmness, completed the business of the first day's session.

The next day a contrite letter arrived from some of the German bishops, but it was too late to avert their doom. Gregory read the resolution of the Council of Worms and the letter of the king before the indignant synod. Excommunication was pronounced on Siegfried of Mainz and all who had signed the acts of the council. Those who had been intimidated into signing were to be deprived unless they made due satisfaction to the pope before St. Peter's Day. The bishops of Lombardy were excommunicated.

But the heaviest missile had yet to be hurled at the head of the greatest offender. After a long and solemn prayer to St. Peter, as whose representative he claimed the power of binding and loosing in heaven and earth, the pope uttered the fearful sentence of deposition and excommunication upon the king : ' For the honour and security of the Church, in the name of the Almighty Triune God, I do prohibit Henry, king, son of Henry the Emperor, from ruling the kingdom of the Teutons and of Italy, and I release all Christians from the oath of allegiance to him which they have taken, or shall take. And inasmuch as he has despised obedience by associating with the excom-

Sentence of deposition and anathema on the king

municate, by many deeds of iniquity, and by spurning the warnings which I have given him for his good, I bind him in the bands of anathema; that all nations of the earth may know that thou art Peter, and that upon thy rock the Son of the living God hath built His Church, and the gates of hell shall not prevail against it.'

Such a tremendous sentence had never before been uttered by any pope. No doubt the same lips had *Situation of the king and the pope* threatened the king of France with deposition; but the threat had not been executed, and the king of France was a far smaller personage than the heir of the Roman Empire. The two greatest potentates in Western Christendom, the spiritual and temporal heads of the Empire, were now locked in a deadly struggle. Yet the deposition of the king by the pope was not so great a shock to the minds of men as the deposition of the pope by the king. Besides the mysterious and awful sanctity of his office, it had never been forgotten that the imperial crown had been originally bestowed by the pope on Charles the Great, and it was a fixed belief that the heir of the empire was not emperor until the pope had placed the imperial crown on his head. If the pope bestowed, could he not withhold? if he elevated, could he not also degrade? But for the king to depose the pope was to treat him like a refractory feudal baron. It meant nothing less than the complete subjection of the ecclesiastical to the secular power; it meant that the emperor, or heir of the empire, could set up and put down popes at his pleasure; that the centre of power was shifted from Italy to Germany; and that Rome was no longer the mistress of the world.

The confidence of Gregory in the justice and final triumph of his cause did not waver for an instant. He invited the faithful to pray that the hearts of his enemies might be turned, and their devices frustrated; but he did not disdain the use of more carnal weapons. He strengthened his military force in Rome; he reopened negotiations with Robert Wiscard and Roger. The bishops in Lombardy, indeed, met at Pavia and anathematised him, but even in Lombardy he had friends. The Patarines were not extinct, and all his partisans found a leader of indomitable, masculine spirit, and large resources, in the great countess Matilda, who, by the recent death of her husband and her mother, was now absolute mistress of her vast inheritance. Her dominions formed a stout bulwark against any attack upon Rome from the north. Nevertheless, Gregory must have waited with anxiety to hear what kind of echo his thunder would awaken on the other side of the Alps.

Had Henry commanded the respect or love of his subjects, no doubt the blow which the pope had dealt would have excited deep indignation. But the reverence which had once been felt for the name of king had been weakened during his minority; and since he came of age neither his private nor public conduct had done much to strengthen it. The nobles had grown hardened in the habit of breaking their oaths of allegiance; and a religious sanction of disloyalty would completely pacify their consciences. The disciples of Clugny had long been preaching the supremacy of Rome, and their teaching now found a congenial soil in Saxony, where the people welcomed a fresh pretext for revolt. Henry was at Utrecht when he received tidings of the sentence pronounced upon him at Rome. He burst into a furious rage, and, with his counsellors, poured forth a torrent of abuse upon the pope; he was a hypocrite, heretic, murderer, perjurer, adulterer; his anathema was null and void, and must be flung back upon his own head. Pibo, the bishop of Toul, formerly chancellor of the king, was commanded to pronounce it; but Pibo shrank from the awful task, and fled from Utrecht by night. William, bishop of Utrecht, had none of his scruples; from the pulpit of his own cathedral he anathematised Gregory: 'The perjured monk who had dared to lift up his hand against the Lord's anointed.' The pious and the timid shuddered at these fearful imprecations invoked upon the head of Christendom, and in the thunderstorm which broke over the city on the same day and struck the cathedral, they read a token of the divine wrath.

The king prepares to retaliate

The king, however, undismayed, summoned a great national council to meet at Worms on Whitsun-day (May 15). Three aged bishops were specially cited, in order to give evidence of the pope's perjury—William of Utrecht, Altwin of Brixen, and Ebbo of Naumburg. The king's letter to Altwin dwells on the grave peril threatened to Church and State by the attempt of Gregory to unite in one hand the two swords—the spiritual and temporal—which God had separated. This is the first example of the image of the two swords, which in later times was so frequently employed.

Henry's plans, however, turned out so ill that men might fairly think that he was pursued by the divine wrath. Altwin of Brixen was seized on his journey

by a Swabian count, and imprisoned; William of
Utrecht suddenly died on April 27; the Council of
<small>Failure of his plans</small> Worms was very scantily attended; few of the
bishops were there and fewer still of the nobles.
Urgent summonses were issued for another council to
be held on June 29 at Mainz, but in the interval most
of the leading nobles withdrew from court, some of
the Saxon prisoners were released or escaped, and the
rebellion was soon in full swing again. The council at
Mainz turned out as signal a failure as the council at
Worms, and at last Henry resolved to negotiate; he
sent conciliatory messages to the nobles, and desired
some of the Saxon prisoners to be brought to Mainz to
treat about terms of ransom. Whilst they were there
a fire broke out, the consequence of a fray between the
servants of the archbishop and the bishop of Bamberg,
and in the confusion all the prisoners escaped. Another
unsuccessful attempt to recover Saxony by attacking
it through Bohemia completed the failure of Henry's
plans. Profoundly dejected, he retreated early in September through the north of Bavaria to Worms. His
position indeed in Germany was becoming most precarious: Saxony was lost; prelates and nobles were
falling away from him, and it was only too plain that,
even in his own kingdom, the power of the pope was
greater than he had reckoned it to be.

While the tempest was thus gathering round Henry
on every side, Gregory had been corresponding with
his friends in Germany and elsewhere. On July 25 he
addressed a letter to all the faithful dwelling in the
Roman Empire; another, on August 25, to Herman,
bishop of Metz; a third, on September 3, to the

'faithful in Christ in the German kingdom.' The import of all the letters is the same. The sentence of excommunication and deposition had not been pronounced until all milder remedies had been tried in vain; precedents are quoted to justify such extreme measures—the deposition of Childeric by pope Zacharias, the repulsion of the emperor Theodosius by Ambrose from the church at Milan. All intercourse with Henry and his counsellors must be avoided, for those who hold communion with him become excommunicate; but if he repents the pope will deal gently with him, for the sake of his incomparable parents. On the other hand, no one must presume to absolve him without the consent of the pope, and, if he remains obstinately impenitent, a new king must be elected.

In September the nobles and prelates held a conference at Ulm, where it was resolved that a diet should be summoned to meet at Tribur on October 16. The pope was informed and approved of the resolution, and appointed Altman, bishop of Passau, and Sieghard, patriarch of Aquileia, to attend it as his legates.

On the appointed day the diet assembled. At Tribur the last emperor of the direct Carolingian line, Charles the Fat, had been deposed (887), and now all Germany seemed prepared to do a like deed. Swabians, Bavarians, Saxons laid aside their discords to combine against the king. Profound respect was shown to the papal legates; the excommunicated bishops, including Siegfried of Mainz, craved and received absolution from them. That the pope had a right to excommunicate the king, and that he had exercised it justly, was soon decided by the council in the affirmative. But the right of the pope to depose, and of the council to make a new election, was not so easily determined. The nobles did not wish to acknowledge an absolute right in the pope to dispose of the throne; but, on the other hand, they did wish to use the papal excommunication as a pretext for electing a new king. Seven days were consumed in debate. Henry, with a few friends, tarried at Oppenheim, on the opposite side of the Rhine. He continually sent messages to the council, promising amendment of his conduct, and offering to surrender the government to the whole body of nobles, if they would leave him the title and insignia of king. The nobles had little faith in his promises, and at first turned a deaf ear to all his proposals. But at last, through the intercession of Hugh, abbot of Clugny, Henry's godfather, they were induced to treat with him. Their terms were deeply humiliating, but the unhappy king was powerless to dispute them. His absolute submission to the pope was demanded; release from excommunication was to be obtained from him alone in person, and if not obtained within twelve months from the date (February 22) on which it had been pronounced, Henry's right to the throne would be irrevocably forfeited. A diet was to be held at Augsburg on February 2, 1077, under the presidency of the pope, to determine the fate of the king and settle the affairs of the Church and kingdom. Meanwhile, Henry was to abide at Speier, deprived of all kingly authority and state, and bereft of all companions but his wife, Dietrich the bishop of Verdun, and a small staff of servants chosen by the nobles. If he adhered to these conditions the nobles promised to conduct him to Rome for his coronation, and to aid him in driving the Normans out of Italy; but if he broke one of them they would renounce all allegiance, and instantly proceed, without waiting even for the pope's sanction, to the election of another king.

Henry retired to Speier and spent about two months there in dreary seclusion, shut out from the services of the Church as well as from the affairs of State. But he was meditating escape from his fetters. He had charged Udo, archbishop of Trier, to convey his submission to Rome, and to inform the pope that he would visit him at Rome to ask absolution. Nothing was further from the wishes of the pope or of the nobles than such a step. The pope was unwilling to be committed to a decision either way before the diet met at Augsburg, where he could preside as arbiter; the nobles feared that, if Henry made terms with him before the diet, they might be unable to elect a new king. But what both sides dreaded actually came to pass. Udo returned with a message from Gregory, declining to receive Henry in Rome, because he was on the point of setting out on his journey, so as to reach Augsburg before the day fixed for the diet. On December 28 he was in Florence; thence he was conducted by the countess Matilda to Mantua, which he reached on January 8, 1077. Here he was waiting for a safe-conduct over the Alps which was to be sent from Germany, when he received the startling news that Henry was already in Italy and had reached Vercelli. The situation was alarming, for Lombardy was still so hostile to the pope that Henry might soon have got an army together for which the troops of Matilda would hardly

[margin: Gregory sets out for Germany, but retires to Canossa.]

have been a match. It was therefore deemed prudent to convey the pope to a place of security; a hasty retreat was made southwards to the Apennines, where Gregory and his friends were lodged in Matilda's strongest castle, the impregnable mountain fortress of Canossa.

CHAPTER XII.

THE MEETING BETWEEN HENRY AND THE POPE AT CANOSSA. THE DIET OF FORCHEIM. RUDOLF OF SWABIA ELECTED KING. JANUARY–MARCH 1077.

THE great aim of Henry was to obtain release from excommunication before the day appointed for the diet at Augsburg. When he was no longer under the ban of the Church the nobles would be deprived of their best excuse for refusing to have intercourse with him, and of their strongest plea for electing a new king. The tidings that the pope declined to receive him in Rome, and was about to set out for Germany, determined him to make a bold move: he would meet the pope on the way.

Henry sets out for Italy.

A few days before Christmas he secretly quitted Speier, accompanied by his wife, with her infant son Conrad, and one faithful attendant. They made their way to Besançon in Upper Burgundy, where they were kindly received by count William, uncle of Henry's mother; and here they spent Christmas-day. Thence they travelled southwards until they entered the dominions of the king's mother-in-law, the marchioness

Adelaide of Susa, who came to meet them, with her son, Amadeus. She agreed to help him on his way to Italy through her territory, but demanded, as the price of her aid, the cession of five rich bishoprics. Necessity extorted a reluctant consent from the king; and then he and his party pushed on to the foot of Mont Cenis. It was a cruel winter—one of the coldest and longest ever known, for the Rhine was frozen from St. Martin's Day (November 11) to the following April. The paths over Mont Cenis were clogged by heavy masses of snow and ice. The ascent was toilsome, but the descent was perilous. The queen and her child were lowered down the icy slopes in rough sledges of ox-hide; men and horses slid and scrambled down as best they might; no human lives were lost, but some horses were killed, others disabled.

At length the weary travellers reached Susa, whence they passed on through Vercelli to Pavia. Lombardy was infested by robbers and distracted by private feuds, and the coming of Henry was heartily welcomed by all who hoped that he would redress disorders, as well as by the anti-papal party.

Henry, however, tarried nowhere, for rest, business, or pleasure, but pressed on towards the goal of his journey—the grim castle in the Apennines. His wife and child, with the bishops and nobles who had gathered round him in his progress through Lombardy, remained at Reggio, about fifteen miles north-east from the castle; only his mother-in-law, her son, and the marquis Azzo of Este accompanied him to Canossa itself. They had to cross a tract of level, fertile country, to the foot of the Apennines, and then to climb

His journey to Canossa.

a long and steep ascent. Fifteen hundred feet or more above the plain, on the neck of one of the mountain-spurs, which are here composed for the most part of black, sterile, volcanic soil, there rises abruptly a craggy mass of grey rock, looking in the distance like a rugged tower. The summit is crowned by some gaunt fragments of the castle of Canossa. It is accessible on one side only, and this was guarded by three walls, of which some vestiges remain, as also of the bridge by which two of them were connected. From the top the vast prospect northwards, over the rich and sunny plain of Lombardy, with its flitting lights and shades, bounded in the far distance by the snowy wall of the Alps, is a strong contrast to the black scene of desolation immediately surrounding the fortress, and the solemn background southwards of bare mountain-peaks. The winter winds rush furiously down the ravines, and over the ridges which divide them. At the present day the ruined castle stands forlorn; the only habitations near it are a few small cottages at the base of the rock, but at the time of which we are writing there were buildings in which a large company could be lodged. For Henry's arrival had been preceded by many of the bishops and laymen whom Gregory had excommunicated. They presented themselves in the garb of suppliants craving absolution. Gregory said that mercy should be shown to those who truly confessed and bewailed their sins, but that the defilements of a long course of sin and disobedience must be purged by the fires of penance. The dejected suppliants said they would submit to any penance he might impose. The prelates were confined for several days in separate chambers with a scanty allowance of food, the laity were dealt with in like manner according to their age and strength. The time allowed for their penance being ended, all were brought before the pope and absolved, after solemn warnings to abstain from intercourse with Henry until he should have made reparation for his offences.

It was January 21, 1077, when Henry arrived at Canossa; the cold was severe, and the snow lay deep. He was lodged at the foot of the castle-steep, and had an interview with the countess Matilda, Hugh, abbot of Clugny, and others, in the chapel of St. Nicolas, of which no traces now remain. Three days were spent in debating terms of reconciliation; Matilda and Hugh interceded with the pope on the king's behalf, but Gregory was inexorable; unless Henry surrendered the crown into the pope's hands the ban should not be taken off. Henry could not stoop so low as this, but he made up his mind to play the part of a penitent suppliant. Early on the morning of January 25 he mounted the winding, rocky path, until he reached the uppermost of the three walls, the one which enclosed the castle yard. And here, before the gateway which still exists, and perpetuates in its name, 'Porta di penitenza,' the memory of this strange event, the king, barefoot, and clad in a coarse woollen shirt, stood knocking for admittance. But he knocked in vain; from morning till evening the heir of the Roman Empire stood shivering outside the fast-closed door. Two more days he climbed the rugged path, and stood weeping and imploring to be admitted, but still the heart of Gregory remained cold and hard as the snow and rocks on which his barefoot suppliant was standing. At last, when he was satisfied that the cup of humiliation had been drained to the dregs, or convinced that further degradation of the king would be impolitic; touched also, it may be, by some feelings of compassion, and by the entreaties of Matilda and the abbot of Clugny, he consented that terms of reconciliation should be drawn up by chosen representatives. The pope's representatives were two cardinal-bishops, two cardinal-priests, two cardinal-deacons, and one sub-deacon; on the king's side were the archbishop of Bremen, the bishops of Osnabrück and Vercelli, the abbot of Clugny, and several laymen of distinction.

By the compact which they drew up the king was to promise that he would attend a meeting of the German nobles whenever it should be called by the pope, and be prepared to retain or forfeit his crown according as the pope, who would preside as arbiter, should pronounce him innocent or guilty of the crimes laid to his charge. Meanwhile he was to lay aside all insignia of royalty, and abstain from all royal functions, and his subjects were absolved from their oaths of fealty; he was to provide a safe-conduct for Gregory, or his legate, across the Alps, and if he proved his innocence he was henceforth to obey the pope in everything which concerned the Church. If he failed to observe any one of these conditions his absolution would be cancelled and the nobles were immediately to elect another king. Henry accepted these hard conditions, and some of the bishops and nobles were required by Gregory to swear upon sacred relics that he would fulfil them.

Then at last the gate of the inner castle was opened

and Henry was admitted into the presence of the stern pontiff whose anathema had for nearly a year blighted his life. With a burst of tears he flung himself at the feet of the pope, crying 'Spare me, holy father, spare me!' The spectators wept, and even the eyes of the austere Gregory were moistened. He raised the king from the ground, gave him his blessing, and conducted him to the chapel[1] where mass was celebrated. A strange tale, which must be accepted, if at all, with caution, is related by some of the chroniclers, that the pope, having broken one of the consecrated wafers in half, called upon God to strike him dead as soon as it had passed his lips if he was guilty of the crimes of which his enemies and Henry had accused him. Having eaten it he remained unharmed, and congratulations burst from the lips of the admiring congregation. Then he offered the other half of the wafer to Henry, and invited him to submit to the same test; if his innocence were thus established his subjects would be reconciled to him, and the tempest of civil war would be hushed for ever. But Henry shrank from the awful test, alleging that his accusers being absent would not believe or be satisfied with such a test, and praying that the whole question might be reserved for a general council, by the decision of which he would faithfully abide. The pope acquiesced, and having finished the service, courteously entertained the king at dinner, and, after some farewell warnings and advice, bade him depart in peace.

He is released from excommunication

And now what had the king and the pope lost or

[1] A solitary marble column with a Romanesque capital probably indicates the site of this chapel

gained by this memorable meeting in the mountain fortress. Henry had stooped to humiliation at Canossa because he saw no other chance of breaking the alliance between his rebellious subjects in Germany and the pope. He had probably hoped to receive, together with absolution, some promise of aid against his adversaries and of the imperial crown. No such promises, however, had been made; on the contrary, he himself had been forced to promise that he would abide by the arbitration of the pope in the questions at issue. He had obtained *bare* absolution, but nothing more; his tenure of the German crown depended on the will of the pope, and of the imperial coronation no mention had been made. And he soon discovered that his reconciliation with Gregory had cost him the good-will of a large and powerful party in Lombardy. All who hoped that he had come to humble the pride of the pope as well as to redress wrongs and disorders, loaded him with the bitterest reproaches for his pusillanimous self-abasement before a tyrannical pontiff; they threatened to enforce his abdication, to elect his son Conrad, to march with him to Rome, and there choose another pope who should crown the boy emperor, and annul all the acts of the detested Gregory. It was in vain that Henry insisted that the safety of his crown had depended upon his getting absolution from the pope before a given day. Some of the nobles withdrew in sullen discontent to their homes, and in his return progress through Lombardy most of the towns withheld the customary honours and hospitalities paid to royal guests.

The triumph of Gregory at Canossa had also revived

the spirits of the Patarine party. Two legates, Gerald of Ostia and Anselm of Lucca, were despatched to Milan and met with a cordial reception; many of the opposition faction expressed contrition, and the whole city seemed to be converted to the papal side. The legates met with some success also in other towns, but when they approached Piacenza, Dionysius, the bishop, attacked them with an armed force and made them both prisoners. Anselm, himself a Lombard, was soon released, but Gerald was detained. Soon afterwards Henry arrived at Piacenza. He was very anxious to receive the crown of Italy either at Milan or Pavia, and had sent a request to Gregory that he would appoint some bishop to perform the coronation. Gregory declined unless his legate was released from imprisonment. The king's mother, who had joined him at Piacenza, urged him to effect the release. But Henry would not interfere: he knew that if he did he should utterly forfeit the support of most of the Lombard bishops, and he did not dare, or was not inclined, to make such a sacrifice. From this date the old distrust between the king and the pope revived: all who were hostile to Gregory gradually rallied round Henry at Pavia. Besides the bishops of Lombardy, most of the German counsellors proscribed by the pope resumed their place and influence: Liemar, archbishop of Bremen; Eppo, bishop of Zeitz; Benno of Osnabrück, Burchard of Lausanne, and Burchard of Basel, and several laymen, of whom the most obnoxious was Ulric of Cosheim.

On the other hand the pope became the centre round which gathered all elements of opposition to the king. Nevertheless, the victory of Gregory at Canossa was not so complete as it appeared to be, because, in fact, he had pushed it too far. Unmindful of the precept 'always make a silver bridge for a retreating enemy,' he had trampled too mercilessly on a fallen foe. There was still so much reverence for the emperor, or heir of the empire, as the highest temporal power ordained by God on earth, that his abject degradation was a shock to Christendom. Some doubted if even the pope could release subjects from their allegiance; some pitied Henry; others dreaded what he might do if driven to desperation. The enemies of the pope in Germany and Rome were still numerous, and they waited their opportunity.

The relation indeed of Gregory to the German nobles had been changed by the event at Canossa. He had repeatedly declared that he would not judge the case except in concert with them; the resolutions at Oppenheim had, in fact, mainly depended for their justification on the king's excommunicate condition, and now this had been removed by the independent action of the pope. A letter which Gregory wrote to the nobles from Canossa just after Henry's visit betrays anxiety to vindicate himself and retain their confidence. He lays great stress upon his own promptness in setting out for Germany, and upon their tardiness in sending an escort for his passage across the Alps, which had enabled Henry to enter Italy before he himself could leave it. He enlarges upon the seemingly humble and penitent state of the king, upon the strong appeals which had been made to his own mercy, and upon the contract by which Henry was bound as the condition of his absolution. Finally, until Gregory himself arrived to take counsel with the nobles, all the questions at issue must be held in suspense.

The letter was received in Ulm, where a small party of the nobles had met (February, 1077) for consultation as soon as the news of the events at Canossa had reached them. They decided that a diet should be held on March 13 at Forcheim. The pope should be invited to attend it, or to send his written judgment through a legate. Henry, himself, was not invited; and Rudolf of Swabia artfully represented to him, through a special messenger, that it would not be prudent for him to appear in Germany until his mother or the pope should have smoothed the way for his reception. The same messenger was sent on to Gregory to urge him to attend the council, but not without obtaining a safe-conduct from the king. Henry did not wish to leave Italy, and he was not inclined to help the pope to intrigue with his enemies in his absence. He, therefore, excused himself from providing the escort, alleging that he was too busy in Italy, and that it would be impossible to get it ready in time. Gregory, therefore, sent two legates to Germany—Bernhard, a cardinal-deacon, and Bernhard, abbot of St. Victor in Marseilles—who were to inform the nobles that he would come if possible; if not, he would pray that they might be guided to a wise decision. The legates themselves were instructed to delay the proceedings, if they could, until he arrived, otherwise they were to yield to the judgment of the nobles.

Henry did nothing to obstruct the plans of his opponents, and the diet met at Forcheim. It was a large, but not a representative, assembly. Of thirteen bishops Bavaria sent only two, Lotharingia one, Swabia not one. The papal legates first conferred privately with the nobles, when they heard all the old accusations against Henry, and expressed their amazement that such a king should have been tolerated so long. The nobles then urged the election of a new king. The legates mildly suggested waiting until the pope should arrive, but confessed they must leave it to the nobles to decide what would be best for the weal of the kingdom. Another private conference was held in the lodging of the archbishop of Mainz. The feeling in favour of electing a new king was general, and with some few dissentients it was agreed that duke Rudolf of Swabia, from his connexion with the royal house, and his sympathy with the papal party, was the most eligible man. The legates, however, insisted that two conditions should be exacted from him—the renunciation of all hereditary claim to the empire for his family after his death, and the permission of free canonical elections to bishoprics. Rudolf assented to these conditions, and on March 15 he was formally elected by the nobles, whose choice was approved by the acclamations of the people. His first anxiety was to receive the approbation of the pope. He sent an envoy to inform Gregory of his election, offering him a safe-conduct if he would come to Germany to regulate the affairs of the Church, and promising to render him faithful obedience. The pope, however, was too cautious to commit himself so hastily, and announced that he should reserve his decision until he had investigated the merits of the rival kings. Meanwhile, on March 26,

CANOSSA 137

Rudolf was crowned at Mainz by the archbishop. Sinister omens occurred: the consecrating oil ran short; the gospel was read by a simoniacal deacon; a fierce brawl broke out between the citizens and the royal servants; the brawl grew into a tumult which was hardly suppressed by Rudolf's knights. He himself had to escape by night like a fugitive, accompanied by archbishop Siegfried, who never returned. Nowhere did Rudolf meet with the reception which he expected. In Swabia and Burgundy, where he had hoped to find his chief support, he and the papal legates were repulsed from Augsburg and Constance by the bishops and townspeople. He spent Whitsunday (June 4) at the abbey of Hirschau, and then quitted Swabia for Saxony, where he found a people ready to welcome him, an army, and a court.

CHAPTER XIII.

THE STRUGGLE IN GERMANY BETWEEN HENRY AND RUDOLF. ELECTION OF AN ANTI-POPE. DEATH OF RUDOLF. DEATH OF GREGORY VII. 1077-85.

As soon as Henry heard of the resolution at Forcheim, he set out from Pavia for Germany, and sent messengers to the pope asking for his support; but Gregory gave the same reply to him as he had given to Rudolf: he would hear both sides and uphold the more righteous. Having spent Easter (April 15) near Aquileia, he crossed the Carinthian

<small>The king returns to Germany, April 1077</small>

Alps (the more westward passes being occupied by Rudolf's friends), and made his way without opposition to Regensberg, where he was cordially received on May 1. The people of Bavaria, Swabia, and Burgundy were ready to fight for him. The bishop of Augsburg and the patriarch of Aquileia worked energetically on his behalf, and few or none of the bishops in Elsass or Lotharingia were actively opposed to him. His enemies were much disconcerted; they had clearly underrated the force of popular attachment to the old imperial line, and overrated the strength of the ecclesiastical party. The cause of Rudolf now entirely depended upon the support of the Saxons, who were hostile to Henry on grounds quite distinct from those of the Gregorians, with whom, indeed, they had no real sympathy.

Henry held a large assembly of his friends at Nuremberg (June 11–13), when it was resolved to collect fresh forces and attack Rudolf in Saxony. The king went to Mainz, and, having mustered a large corps there of burghers from the Rhenish towns, he took up an almost unassailable position on the lower Neckar, and waited there for reinforcements from Bavaria and Bohemia.

As soon as Gregory had heard of Henry's movements, he sent instructions to his legates to demand a safe-conduct for himself from both parties, that he might go to Germany and arbitrate between their claims. Whichever party refused the escort was to be anathematised. But neither of the two was inclined to accede to his demands. Rudolf's side was offended because the pope had not immediately recognised his election. Henry was angry with him because his legates, by openly

THE LAST YEARS OF GREGORY VII. 139

espousing the cause of Rudolf, had violated the compact made at Canossa.

Gregory now abandoned his projected visit to Germany, and retired from Lombardy to Rome. The nobles made an attempt to bring the strife to an end without bloodshed. It was agreed that an armistice should be made until a great diet, which was to meet on November 1 for the settlement of the question. Whoever did not observe the armistice was to be reckoned a common enemy. Henry, however, took little heed of it, and busied himself with warlike pre-

The pope's legate declares Rudolf king

parations. Whilst he was rambling up and down his dominions, Rudolf's authority was undisputed in Saxony; but the proposed diet came to nothing, and on November 12, at Goslar, the legate, cardinal Bernhard, pronounced the ban upon Henry, and declared Rudolf to be the legitimate king. The archbishop of Mainz and seven suffragans also published the anathema. Rudolf celebrated Christmas at Goslar with great pomp, and messengers were despatched to the pope imploring him to ratify the act of his legate. But Henry also sent two envoys, and his power was too great to be despised. Bavaria, Swabia, Bohemia, Lombardy, Burgundy were all on his side, and Lotharingia and Franconia were not actively hostile.

In fact, since the meeting at Canossa, Henry's prospects had improved, while Gregory was becoming every

Gregory's difficulties and indecision

day more entangled in a web of difficulties and dangers. He, who seemed to hold the fate of the German kingdom and the Roman empire in his hand, could not venture upon a bold line of action in any direction. In Italy he was hampered on the one side by a strong adverse party in Lombardy, and on the other by the suspicious movements of the Normans, Robert Wiscard having seized Benevento on the death of duke Landulf VI. without an heir. In Germany the pope had no material force at his disposal to aid either side, and the two seemed so nearly balanced that he shrank from declaring positively for either, and took refuge in an equivocating policy. He neither ratified nor repudiated the decision of his legate in favour of Rudolf, and he reopened negotiations with Henry. The death of the empress Agnes at the close of the year 1077 and of Gerald of Ostia, one of his most trustworthy legates, increased his difficulties in dealing with German affairs. He now relinquished all hope of settling the strife between Henry and Rudolf in person; but after the Lenten synod at Rome (1078) he sent fresh legates to Germany with instructions to hold a council in which they were to arbitrate between the rivals, and, if possible, arrange terms of peace. It is significant of his anxiety to concilate the German clergy at this crisis, that the prohibition of lay investiture was not repeated at the synod, and many bishops were kindly received who had accepted the ring and staff at the hands of Henry. Rudolf and his party were bitterly disappointed and irritated at the results of this synod. Their envoys had been received in secret; Henry's in public; and the new legates were conducted to Germany by Udo, archbishop of Trier, who was known to be an advocate of Henry's cause. The Saxon nobles wrote a letter to the pope accusing him of ingratitude, and of causing misery to the country by his vacillation.

For two more weary years (1078-1080) the balance wavered between the two contending sides; the pope hesitating to throw his weight into either scale. He wrote letters demanding a diet at which his legates were to arbitrate, and anathematising all who should hinder it; but the diet did not meet, and war broke out. On August 7, 1078, Henry defeated a portion of Rudolf's army at Melrichstadt by the river Streu in Franconia. Envoys from both sides were heard at a Lateran council in November, but received ambiguous answers.

Henry's victory at Melrichstadt, 1078

At the Lent synod in 1079 the pope was urged to renew the anathema on Henry, but the final decision was again postponed to Whitsuntide, nor did it even then take place. At length, after many fruitless embassies to Rome, and proposals for a council which was always frustrated or deferred, the armies of the rival kings met (January 27) near the river Unstrut in Thuringia, and after a fierce and bloody battle Henry was totally defeated.

His defeat near the Unstrut, 1080

Rudolf and his partisans now determined to force the pope to a decision in their favour. They sent a letter to him severely reproaching him for having prolonged the strife in Germany by his irresolution, and demanding his recognition of a divine decision in the victory with which the arms of Rudolf had been blessed. Gregory now perceived that, if he would retain any influence in Germany, the decisive step must be taken.

The Lent synod at Rome in the first week of March was largely attended. Fifty archbishops and bishops were present, and a host of abbots and clergy, chiefly from Italy and Gaul. The strongest decrees ever framed against lay investiture were now issued. Emperor, king, duke, or count who persisted in the practice would be liable to excommunication. The clergy and people were to make free elections to ecclesiastical offices, and if their choice was perverted by secular influence, the appointment was to lapse to the metropolitan or the pope. A long list of persons excommunicated was then read, the most conspicuous being the archbishops Tedald of Milan and Wibert of Ravenna. The Normans were threatened with the same fate if they dared to make any further encroachments upon Benevento, Fermo, or the duchy of Spoleto. Then the envoys of Rudolf had an audience, and made the worst of Henry's offences—his seizure of the kingdom after he had been deposed, his violent ejection of bishops and abbots, whom he replaced with nominees of his own, his incessant efforts to frustrate the meeting which the pope had called for the settlement of the strife, the misery, and bloodshed caused by the war which he had provoked. Their tale of wrongs was patiently heard; the envoys of Henry, on the contrary, were hardly permitted to speak.

Synod at Rome, March 1080

On the last day of the synod (March 7) Gregory pronounced judgment. After invoking St. Peter and St. Paul as witnesses of his truth, of the reluctance with which he had occupied the papal throne, and of the countless troubles which he had suffered on behalf of the Church, he briefly reviewed and justified his action during the past four years. He had restored Henry to the communion of the Church, but not to his throne; he had purposed

The pope renews the ban upon Henry

to decide that question at a council in Germany; and since Rudolf had been elected without his advice or consent, his constant aim had been to bring about a meeting at which he might examine and adjudicate upon the rival claims of the two kings. But such a council had been perpetually thwarted by Henry, who had brought misery upon the Church and kingdom by sacrilegious violence and war. Wherefore he declared the said Henry and all his partisans excommunicate, deprived him of the kingdoms of Germany and Italy, forbad all the faithful to obey him, and absolved from their oath all who had sworn or should swear allegiance to him: he bestowed the kingdom upon Rudolf, and absolved from their sins all who should faithfully adhere to him. 'So act, I pray you, most holy fathers, that all the world may know that if ye can bind and loose in Heaven, ye can also give or take away kingdoms, dukedoms, principalities, and all other possessions according to the merits of each man. For ye have often taken away patriarchates, archbishoprics, and bishoprics from the wicked, to bestow them on the good. And if ye judge in spiritual things, ought ye not to be deemed able to judge in worldly things? Let your sentence against Henry be speedily executed, and may he be so turned to repentance that his spirit may be saved in the day of the Lord!'

Having at last taken the decisive step, the confidence of Gregory in his divine authority seemed to increase; and he hazarded a prediction that before the day of SS. Peter and Paul (June 29) Henry would have lost either his life or his throne.

But, as after the humiliation of Henry at Canossa, so

now, the blow seemed to recoil upon him who gave it. There was a revulsion of feeling in favour of the king. His party in Italy and Germany became stronger and more compact. Ravenna and the Romagna became centres of an organised movement against the Pope and the Patarines. Most of the German bishops rallied round Henry. At Bamberg, where he spent Easter, many of them renounced obedience to Gregory, and at Whitsuntide an assembly of nineteen bishops and several lay lords in Mainz resolved to depose him and elect another pope. Huzman, bishop of Speier, addressed a letter to the Lombards, and Dietrich of Verdun addressed another to the nobles and clergy throughout the empire, full of fierce denunciations of Gregory and earnest appeals for help to get rid of the turbulent monk. On June 25 a large assembly was held at Brixen, where he was deposed by a decree signed by twenty-seven bishops out of thirty, and anathema was pronounced on him, and on Rudolf, and all their adherents.

Wibert of Ravenna was unanimously elected antipope the next day. He was a man of high birth, handsome presence, dignified manners, good abilities, and irreproachable morals. He had spent much time at the court of Henry III.,

<small>Wibert elected antipope, June 26, 1080</small>

and had administered Italian affairs, as chancellor of the kingdom, during the minority of Henry IV. For a short time after his elevation to the see of Ravenna he had been on friendly terms with Gregory, but a dispute had soon arisen about rights of jurisdiction over Imola, and other matters, after which he became the head of the anti-papal party in Lombardy. Such a complete schism in the Holy Roman Empire had

THE LAST YEARS OF GREGORY VII. 145

never yet been witnessed: there were two rival kings, and two rival popes, and only war could decide the issue of the contest.

The festival of SS. Peter and Paul arrived, but Gregory's prediction of Henry's downfall had not been fulfilled. He was not only alive, but vigorously preparing for an attack upon Rudolf. The pope saw the urgent need of securing some military aid, and he sought it from the Norman chief whom he had hitherto denounced and excommunicated as an invader of Roman territory. Through the help of Desiderius, the abbot of Monte Cassino, a meeting was arranged at Ceprano between Gregory and Robert Wiscard. Robert became a tributary of the Pope, and took an oath to defend him and his legitimate successors against all unlawful usurpers. He was then invested, as duke of Apulia, Calabria, and Sicily, with the gift of a consecrated banner. It was commonly reported that the pope offered the imperial throne to Robert, but this seems scarcely credible, and Robert's ambition just then was directed rather to the new than to the old Rome. His daughter was married to the son of the Eastern emperor Michael VII.; but Michael had just been deposed, and Robert was anxious to drive out the usurper, Nicephorus Botaniates, and restore Michael to the throne, or occupy it himself. Gregory reckoned on his partisans in Germany, especially Altman, bishop of Passau, and the dukes Welf and Berthold, to counteract the movements of Henry, whilst with the aid of the Normans he hoped to make an attack on the schismatics in Lombardy. He appealed for help, but in vain, to William the Conqueror and the king of Denmark; he summoned all the faithful in Italy to aid in recovering Ravenna for St. Peter out of the hands of the ungodly. The expedition was to be made in September, but the Normans did not come to the muster, and, in fact, he had no powerful ally in Italy on whom he could rely except the great countess Matilda, and even she was just then crippled by a rebellion amongst her vassals. Gregory, however, quailed not; he staked his hopes upon a decisive battle to be fought in Germany. The battle was to be, but the issue was not to fulfil his expectation.

On October 15, the armies of the rival kings met on the banks of the river Saale in Saxony. After a long and bloody contest Henry was defeated, but Rudolf was mortally wounded, and the remainder of the year was wasted by his party in disputing who should be elected to succeed him. Henry prepared meanwhile for a visit to Italy early in the following year, to secure, as he hoped, the consecration of Wibert as pope, and his own coronation.

Battle on the Saale. Death of Rudolf, 1080

In March, he set out, crossed the Brenner, spent Easter at Verona, and thence hastened to Milan, where he probably received the iron crown. From Milan he went to Ravenna, and having raised some additional forces in the March of Ancona, he advanced towards Rome, ravaging the territories of Matilda on the way. It was reported that he had made terms with Robert Wiscard; at any rate Robert paid no heed to Gregory's appeal for aid, although it was urged by Desiderius, the abbot of Monte Cassino. The pope sent messengers to his friends in Germany, imploring succour, but help came neither from the north nor from the south,

Henry goes to Italy, 1081

THE LAST YEARS OF GREGORY VII. 147

and his friends in Rome advised him to make terms with Henry. But the intrepid pope declared that he would rather die than yield; he expressed confidence that the Roman people, at least, would stand by him; and in this expectation he was not deceived.

The walls were repaired and manned. On Friday before Whitsunday, Henry, with a small force, appeared before Rome. He had flattered himself that the Romans would welcome his coming and expel the pope, but he found them prepared for an obstinate resistance. The holy festival had to be kept outside the walls. Mass was celebrated in a tent, and some sorry pretence of crowning the king was made. Here he tarried till the end of June, when an outbreak of fever warned him to retreat, and he turned his back upon Rome, more humiliated and discomfited than when he left Canossa. There the door had at last been opened to him, but the gates of the imperial city had remained obstinately closed. His repulse in Italy, of course, emboldened his opponents in Germany, who at last elected Herman, brother to count Conrad of Luxemburg, as successor to Rudolf, and crowned him at Goslar.

Reaches Rome, May 21, but is repulsed

Henry, however, had still a strong party in Italy. He spent the remainder of the year amongst the northern towns, bestowing privileges on many of them, in return for which they promised him support against the countess Matilda. In fact, only Florence remained quite steadfast to her, but her indomitable energy and the ability and zeal of her confidential adviser, Anselm, bishop of Lucca, not only enabled her to save her own dominions, but even to send some aid to the pope.

In the spring of the next year, Henry returned to

Rome with a larger force; he made appeals and specious promises to the citizens, but in vain; then he laid siege to the city, and the siege was gradually turned into a blockade. Provisions and money became very scarce. Matilda melted down the plate of the church at Canossa to relieve the pope's necessities, and no succour came from any quarter. Robert Wiscard was on the other side of the Adriatic; the anti-king was prevented from leaving Germany by the death of Otto of Nordheim, his vice-gerent in Saxony. Henry, after revisiting Lombardy, returned next year with augmented forces and succeeded at length in taking the greater part of the city, except the castle of St. Angelo, where Gregory himself was lodged, and on June 3 the royal army lay encamped around St. Peter's. Again the friends of Gregory implored him in mercy to the distressed city to make terms, but again the dauntless pope refused: 'Let the king lay down his crown and make satisfaction to the Church;' on no other terms would he treat with him. Henry exacted a promise from the Roman nobles that they would force Gregory to crown him by November 1, or elect a new pope; and then he withdrew to spend the summer in Lombardy.

His second attack, 1082

His third attack, 1083, partially successful

At last Robert Wiscard found it to be his interest to befriend the pope. Rebellion had broken out in Apulia, fomented by the Eastern emperor, Alexius, who urged Henry to support it, sent him supplies of money to help him against Rome, and sought the hand of Henry's daughter, Agnes, for his own nephew and probable successor. Early in February Henry made an incursion into

He is crowned by the anti-pope, Easter, 1084

Apulia, with part of his army, meeting little resistance; in March he was again in Rome, and on the 21st, accompanied by his wife, the anti-pope, and a large number of German and Italian bishops and nobles, he took possession of the Lateran palace. Here a synod was held, which deposed and excommunicated Gregory; on Palm Sunday Wibert was consecrated with the title of Clement III., and on Easter day (March 31), he crowned Henry and his wife in the Church of St. Peter.

In both ceremonials precedents were followed as far as circumstances permitted; but the Gregorians maintained that the whole proceedings were irregular, and therefore invalid. Wibert was consecrated by the excommunicated bishops of Modena and Arezzo; no blessing could be conveyed by their hands, and as Wibert was not pope, Henry, crowned by his hands, was not emperor.

Henry and his pope were masters of nearly all Rome, but it was a brief and sorry triumph. The alliance of Henry with the Eastern emperor, and his attack upon Apulia, had thoroughly exasperated Robert Wiscard, and he now resolved to seize Rome. Leaving his army at Durazzo, under the command of his son, Bohemund, he crossed to Italy, and collected a motley force made up of Normans, Lombards, Apulians, and Saracens, amounting to 30,000 foot and 6,000 horse, with which, early in May, he advanced upon Rome. Henry was not prepared to face such a host under such a leader, and, promising to return ere long with rich rewards for the valiant, he quitted the city, May 21, and hastened through Verona to Germany.

On May 27 Robert arrived before Rome, and encamped by the aqueduct of Nero, before St. John's Gate. Early next morning some friends inside Rome secretly opened the Pincian and Flaminian gates, the troops rushed in, poured in a mighty torrent over the Campus Martius, shouting 'Wiscard! Wiscard!' and, having crossed St. Peter's bridge, speedily captured the castle of St. Angelo, from which Gregory was conducted to the Lateran palace. Rome now lay at the mercy of the conquerors. Naturally in such a large, mixed host, many of the soldiers were ferocious and insolent; scuffles broke out between them and the citizens, in one of which a Norman vassal of Robert's was killed. Robert permitted, if he did not order, the fearful vengeance which ensued; the city was abandoned to fire and pillage; the people to slaughter and outrage. Some of the principal churches were spared at the intercession of Gregory, but he had the mortification of seeing half the city reduced to ruins, and thousands of the inhabitants carried away as captives. The miserable remnant cursed the pope and his deliverer, and, in the words of a contemporary anarchist, the cruelty of the Normans gained more hearts for the emperor than 100,000 gold pieces.

Sack of Rome by Robert Wiscard's troops

About the end of June Robert prepared to move southwards with the bulk of his army. Gregory had to be content with a vague promise of indemnity for the injuries inflicted upon the city, which he now quitted never to return. Accompanied by some cardinals, and a few Roman nobles, he was conducted first to Monte Cassino, where they were received with

Gregory quits Rome

much honour, by Desiderius the abbot; thence he proceeded to Benevento, and finally to Salerno.

The anti-pope Clement, who had retired to Tivoli, now came back to Rome, celebrated Christmas there, and gathered a little court around him of such bishops, clergy, and nobles as were hostile to Gregory; but he was of small account without the emperor, and Henry having got his crown had no mind to return to Rome. To reign in Rome, indeed, could have been but little joy for either emperor or pope. The most renowned and revered city in the world was a miserable ghost of her former self. More than ten years after the catastrophe, it is described by one who visited it as a scene of melancholy desolation; towers and castles, standing out gaunt and grim amidst the wreck of palaces and churches; while those churches which still remained were surrounded with such high, strong walls that they looked more like fortresses than Christian temples.

Rome lay in ruins, and the pope was in exile. His bodily powers were beginning to decay, but his spirit remained unshaken to the last. He was as imperious at Salerno as at Rome, as confident in the justice and ultimate triumph of his cause. A synod was held in which he hurled anathemas once more at Henry and Wibert. Legates were sent to Germany and France to stir up the courage of his adherents, and bearing with them a circular letter addressed to the faithful, in which they were commanded, as they valued their salvation, to hasten to the rescue of the Holy Roman Church, the mother and mistress of all churches. The legates were also to remind them of the annual tribute, which had been regularly paid to Rome in the days of Charles the

Great. In fact they were to try and muster an army, and levy a subsidy from Christendom; but they met with scanty success, and the only resources upon which Gregory could rely were those of Matilda and the Normans. In July, 1084, the troops of the countess had surprised and defeated a force raised by Henry in Lombardy on its way to aid the anti-pope at Rome. If Gregory could have returned to the city immediately after this victory he might have been reinstated, but Robert Wiscard was on the other side of the Adriatic, busy again with his eastern projects, and preparing to winter in Epirus. It was clear that Gregory would not be conducted back to Rome by the Normans, and in the spring of the following year it was equally clear that his end was not far off.

On May 18 he summoned the little band of cardinals who had followed him into exile, and told them he Death of Gregory, May 25, 1085 had but eight days to live. In reviewing the course of his eventful life he said that he had only one supreme consolation—the consciousness that he had at least loved right and hated wrong. And raising his eyes to heaven, he bade his friends dismiss their fears concerning what should befall them when he was gone, seeing he was about to depart to the other world, where, with fervent prayer, he would commend their cause to God. They then asked him to intimate his wishes respecting the election of his successor. He named Desiderius, abbot of Monte Cassino, Anselm, bishop of Lucca, Otto, bishop of Ostia, and Hugh, archbishop of Lyons, as the worthiest men, suggesting a certain preference for Desiderius as being nearest at hand. They questioned him concerning the absolution of the excommunicated. 'Henry and Wibert,' he replied, ' with all who by counsel and deed have supported their impious designs, I absolve not; all others I freely bless who hold fast the belief that I exercise this power as the representative of St. Peter and St. Paul.'

On the 25th the great pope was no more; just before breathing his last he repeated the words, 'I have loved righteousness and hated iniquity—therefore I die in exile.' ' Nay,' said one of the bishops, ' in exile thou canst not die, who as vicar of Christ and His Apostles, hast received the nations for thine inheritance, and the utmost parts of the earth for thy possession.'

He was buried at Salerno, in the Church of St. Matthew, which he had consecrated to receive the remains, recently discovered, as it was supposed, of the Evangelist. Two hundred years afterwards a sumptuous chapel was built over the grave, where the remains rested until they were translated by pope Paul V., in 1609, to a spot beneath the high altar. His name was inserted in the Calendar in 1584 by Gregory XIII., and from that time his day began to be publicly celebrated at Salerno, but Benedict XIII., in 1728, was the first pope who ordered it to be generally observed.

The last words of Gregory—'I have loved righteousness and hated iniquity'—were no more than the truth. Character and aims of Gregory He had no selfish or sordid aims; the moral purification of the Church, its organisation as a great spiritual empire under one supreme head, and its emancipation, for this purpose, from all secular control—this was the ideal for which he lived. The dying words of one of our own archbishops, 'Pro ecclesiâ Dei, pro ecclesiâ Dei,' might well stand as the motto of Gregory's life; the victories of the Church were his joys, her defeats his sorrows. The papal claims, as he is supposed to have conceived them, are formulated in a document preserved amongst his letters. Whether it was really framed in his time or under his direction may be a matter of doubt, but, at least, it contains little or nothing which is not involved in the principles which he actually maintained. The digest consists of twenty-seven brief propositions, asserting, amongst other rights, that the pope alone is the universal pontiff; he is the supreme and irresponsible arbiter in all questions of right and wrong, he alone can depose and reinstate bishops, and of all bishops his legates take precedence. He only can wear the imperial insignia, he alone can depose emperors, and absolve subjects from their allegiance to wicked sovereigns. All princes should kiss his feet.

It is easy for us, looking at them in the light of later history, to denounce these claims as extravagant and mischievous; but as things then were the absolute independence of the Church from all secular control seemed to many besides Gregory essential to her purification, and, indeed, her existence as a spiritual power. The conflict between the Church and the world in that age meant a struggle to determine whether the feudal or the ecclesiastical, the military or the religious should be the dominant force in European society. The issue was put on the strife about investiture. The feudal aristocracy were too often fierce, insolent, licentious; and if prelates were to be placed under the heels of such men it was impossible that they should do their duty as guides and guardians of the moral and spiritual life, and the whole conception of their office would become degraded. But investiture as then practised did involve these consequences, for it was made with the ring and staff, the emblems of spiritual marriage and authority; investiture by these signified the bestowal, not merely of the temporalities, but of the office itself; it meant that the receiver became the absolute vassal—in technical feudal language, 'the man'—of him who thus invested him.

Nor may we fairly blame Gregory for the evils which may seem to us to have sprung out of the ordinance of clerical celibacy. Clerical marriage, we must remember, was contrary to the sentiment of the age, and had long been condemned by the law of the Church: by canon law it was not marriage at all, but mere concubinage, and men who had so far done violence to their conscience as to break the law of the Church, were not very scrupulous in transgressing again, and were often unfaithful to their concubines. The marriage of the clergy, moreover, tended, not only to secularise them, but to form them into a kind of hereditary caste, with strong local sympathies, weakening the tie between them and Rome, and thus hindering one of Gregory's chief aims, which was to organise the whole Church on one type under one supreme head. In the network of feudalism which covered Europe, parcelling it out amongst a multitude of rulers infinitely graduated in rank and power, the unity of the Church would have been fatally impaired had there not been a central power to hold it together, maintaining everywhere, as nearly as possible, the same standard of doctrine, the same form of worship, the same religious customs and moral principles. How Gregory played the part of such a central power can best be understood by a study of his letters.

They are addressed to all kinds of persons, in all parts of Western Christendom, and are concerned with a vast variety of subjects: disputes between bishops and abbots, claims of rival candidates for bishoprics, rights of metropolitans, the protection of monastic property from cupidity and violence, questions about marriages within forbidden degrees, or the penalties to be exacted for moral offences. An unaffected piety, an intimate knowledge of Scripture, a zealous anxiety for the advancement of pure morality are conspicuous in all his letters. Even a Saracen emir is addressed as a friend on the strength of his kindness to some Christians and his belief in the one true God. Kings, nobles, bishops, abbots, all who bear rule of any kind, are warned to be mindful of their trust, and do their duty, actuated neither by fear nor by favour, neither by love of money nor desire of vain-glory. His tone, however, varies according to the character and condition of the person addressed: to intimate friends he is tender; to sinners, like Philip I. of France, severely stern; to William of England more than to any other sovereign he is respectful and even complimentary. Once, indeed, he ventured to ask too much from him: he demanded fealty as well as 'more punctual payment of Peter's pence.' The strong-willed conqueror taught him not to presume again: 'Peter's pence he would pay, for his predecessors had paid it; fealty they had not paid, and it never should be paid by him.' Yet to all, whatever their rank and power might be, Gregory writes as a spiritual father who has authority to rebuke, to admonish, to command his children. The close connexion between the Papacy and all parts of the spiritual empire was further maintained, not only by letters and legates, but by the attendance of bishops at the synods in Rome. Neglect to obey citations to these synods was a heinous offence, visited, if too often repeated, with the penalties of suspension or excommunication. Lanfranc did not escape sharp reprimands for remissness in this duty; and the most severe rebuke which Gregory ever dared administer to the Conqueror was for hindering some bishops from leaving his dominions to visit Rome. The spiritual father demanded strict obedience from even the greatest of his sons.

Thus did Gregory read his commission. It was not the habit of men in that age to look very far ahead and speculate about the remote consequences of their acts: what they believed to be right, or good, or desirable, this they commonly pursued with simple faith and eagerness. Gregory was no doubt hurried sometimes by excess of zeal into acts of indefensible severity, and sometimes, in moments of perplexity, he stooped to unworthy subterfuges; but his aim was a noble one: he never lost sight of it; by his transcendent genius he came near to attaining it, and left the more complete attainment possible for his successors.

Two months after his death another man, hardly less wonderful, died, whose career had in many strange ways been linked with his. Robert Wiscard, not easily moved to tears, is said to have wept when he heard of the pope's death. He was then preparing for a great expedition to Constantinople. Early in July he set sail, sickened with fever on the

Death of Robert Wiscard, July 17, 1085

voyage, was landed in Corfu, and died in the seventieth year of his age. The claim of his son Roger to the dukedom of Apulia was contested by a half-brother Bohemund, and Gisulf of Salerno tried to regain that principality. The archbishopric of Salerno fell vacant about this time: Sigelgaita, Robert's widow, tried to get it for a relation of the deceased primate, who was attached to her family, but her design was opposed by Gisulf and the cardinals who had been with Gregory. Sigelgaita and Roger then broke off their intercourse with the Gregorian party, and released all the prisoners who had been brought from Rome.

CHAPTER XIV.

SHORT PONTIFICATE OF VICTOR III. ELECTION OF URBAN II. THE COUNCIL OF CLERMONT. PROCLAMATION OF THE FIRST CRUSADE. URBAN'S RECEPTION AT ROME. 1086–96.

THE Gregorian party were much divided in opinion respecting the best course of action to be taken after the death of their leader. Some held that the welfare of the Church depended upon adhering closely to his policy: others that the cause of reform itself would be imperilled by insisting rigidly upon it.

Rome was in the hands of the imperialists, and it was not till the spring of the year after the death of Gregory, the anti-pope having retired to Ravenna for a time, that the cardinals, protected by Cencius Frangipane, ventured to meet in Rome. Anselm of Lucca, one of Gregory's nominees for the Papacy, was dead, Otto of Ostia was on the point of

Desiderius elected pope, May 24, 1086

SHORT PONTIFICATE OF VICTOR III. 159

being elected, but some objections being raised there was a sudden burst of feeling in favour of Desiderius, abbot of Monte Cassino: he was forcibly seized and proclaimed pope on Whitsunday (May 24), with the title of Victor III. Desiderius was a man of rank, ability, and conciliatory disposition, and he had the good-will of the Normans; but he was an old man, deeply attached to his monastery, and he shrank from grappling with the disorders in Rome. Four days after his election, being yet unconsecrated, he quitted the city, put off his papal robes at Terracina, and retired to Monte Cassino. In the ensuing Lent, stung by the reproaches of the more severe Gregorians, who accused him of complicity with the imperialists, he returned to Rome, conducted by Jordan of Capua, and, under the protection of his troops, was consecrated in St. Peter's. The countess Matilda had succeeded in occupying the Trasteverine quarter with her troops, but after a fierce struggle the imperialists got possession of St. Peter's. Sick in body and weary of strife, Victor again retreated to Monte Cassino. His last public act was to hold a synod at Benevento (August), where the decrees against simony and lay investiture were promulgated. On the third day after his return to Monte Cassino he died, and was buried in the abbey which he loved so well.

When Victor died, Rome was in the hands of the Wibertians, and six months elapsed before it could be decided where the election of a new pope should take place. At last Terracina was selected. A large number of cardinals and bishops assembled there on March 8 in person or by proxy, and the Romans were represented by their prefect. A three days' fast was kept, and on

March 12 the election was held, when there was a vast preponderance of votes for Otto of Ostia. Otto was a Frenchman who had been trained at Clugny, and had all the qualities most characteristic of that school—ascetic piety and zeal for the reformation of the Church combined with considerable worldly wisdom and tact. In common with most of the Clugniacs he sympathised with the principles and aims of Gregory, but disapproved of the vehemence with which he attempted to enforce them.

<small>Otto, bishop of Ostia, elected pope (Urban II. 1088)</small>

Otto was consecrated at Terracina a few days after his election, taking the title of Urban II. His first act was to despatch letters to the countess Matilda, and to his friends in Germany and Gaul, informing them of his election and of his intention to walk in the footsteps of Gregory; 'what he rejected I reject, what he condemned I condemn, what he loved I embrace.' To England, where William the Red had just succeeded his father, he sent a special messenger, with a friendly letter to Lanfranc, imploring him to exhort the king to support the Roman Church in her distress, and to be punctual in the payment of Peter's pence. Lanfranc, however, regarded the strife for the papal throne with seeming indifference, and would not commit the Church of England to a decision in favour of either claimant.

The election of Urban nearly coincided with several valiant and successful efforts to force back the tide of Mohammedan conquest. Roger had driven the Arabs out of Sicily; the Pisans had vanquished their piratical fleet; Alphonso VI. of Castille had won great victories over them in Spain. And all these champions of the faith espoused the side of Urban. Matilda also was again dominant in North Italy. Nevertheless the party of the anti-pope kept a firm hold upon Rome, and after two or three attempts to dislodge his rival, and a brief and precarious residence on the island in the Tiber, Urban abandoned the city in 1090, and for the next three years sojourned chiefly in Norman territory, holding his synods in Benevento.

But, although shut out from the capital, it was in Italy that Urban found the chief resources for carrying on his contest with the emperor. Henry's most powerful adversary was Welf, duke of Bavaria, whose son, a youth of eighteen, had lately married the countess Matilda. Her motive in contracting this strange alliance was to secure the aid of the Welfs for the pope; their hope was to gain possession of her vast inheritance, not knowing that she had already devoted it to the Papacy. Henry saw that his principal aim must be to crush the united forces of Matilda and the Welfs. About the end of the year 1087, he sent his son Conrad into Lombardy, who was so successful in defeating the troops commanded by Matilda's husband that in 1089 she concluded a truce, which was to last till Easter 1090.

State of affairs in Italy

Near the end of March Henry himself set out for Italy, and arrived at Verona on April 10. On the issue of his contest with the great countess depended not only his own position in Germany, but the future of Italy and the papacy. If Matilda and the Welfs were overthrown, all Lombardy would lie at the mercy of the conqueror, Clement the anti-pope would be securely established in Rome, and Urban would be

The emperor goes to Italy, 1090

either entirely confined to the south of the peninsula, or would have to seek refuge in France.

The emperor reached Mantua the capital of Matilda's dominions without a check, but here he encountered a stout and stubborn resistance. For eleven months Mantua defied the besiegers, and it was only through treachery that it fell at last. Henry spent Easter there, gathered a court around him, and gradually reduced all the castles of Matilda north of the Po save Piedena and Nogara. She retreated to her strongholds in the Apennines, and from them protected, as well as she could, the districts of Reggio and Modena.

<small>Mantua taken, April 10, 1091</small>

The prospect became a very gloomy one for Urban. Even amongst the Normans his position was precarious: his friend Jordan of Capua had just died, and his death was followed by a revolt of the Capuans against his son Richard. In Germany also the imperial fortunes seemed to be reviving. Even Welf began to think of making terms.

Henry spent Christmas in Mantua, and remained there, keeping the 'Truce of God,' until Whitsuntide (1092). In June he set to work again to subdue the castles of Matilda, who was reduced to great straits. She held a council of bishops and abbots; some of them advised surrender, but the hermit John of Canossa fiercely denounced any peace with Henry. Compromise with the oppressor of the Church would be sin against the Holy Ghost. The judgment of the holy man commended itself to the intrepid spirit of the countess, and all thought of negotiation was abandoned. Henry now attacked the fortresses in the Apennines, and assailed Canossa. Gladly

<small>Henry's war with the countess Matilda</small>

would he have wiped out the memory of his humiliation there by a triumphant victory. But it was not to be: the garrison, under cover of a dense mist in the early morning, fell upon the imperial troops and captured a standard, which was hung up as a precious trophy in the chapel of the castle. Baffled and vexed, Henry retired north of the Po.

The partisans of Matilda and the Welfs were elated, and a league to resist Henry was formed between Milan, Piacenza, Lodi, and Cremona. The first act of the league was to occupy all the passes of the Alps, thus cutting off Henry's communication with his friends in Germany.

But a bitterer calamity than any which had yet befallen him was now impending. His eldest son Conrad, Revolt of a handsome youth of nineteen, easy of disposition and affable in manners, was a general favourite in Germany and Italy. Matilda and her friends conceived the project of setting up the son as king in Italy against the father. And Conrad was weak enough to yield to the artful flattery of his tempters. Henry was keeping Easter at Pavia when he received the terrible tidings of his son's revolt. His life had been a perpetual struggle with adversities, and he had faced them all bravely, but now for the first time his fortitude gave way. He fell into a state of profound dejection, and was scarcely restrained by his friends from putting an end to his life. He withdrew eastwards behind the Adige into the friendly territory of the Eppensteiner, and there spent a long season of dreary, helpless inactivity, while town after town in Lombardy declared for his unnatural son. Matilda and the

Patarines recovered their supremacy from the Alps to the Tiber. Conrad was crowned by the archbishop of Milan, first at Monza, and afterwards at Milan in the church of St. Ambrose. In November Urban came back to Rome; the anti-pope was with Henry, and regarded their cause as so utterly lost that he offered to abdicate, but to this Henry would not consent.

And now one more calamity was to be added to the load of misery already piled upon the emperor's head. His fond and faithful wife Bertha had died in 1087; a year later he had married Praxedis, the daughter of a Russian duke, and widow of Henry, count of the northern march. The story of his relations with this second wife, if not too obscure, is too revolting to be investigated. She had for some time been kept in close durance, from which she now contrived to escape, and seeking refuge with Matilda poured into her ear a tale of wrongs, accusing her husband of forcing her to lead a life of odious vice. 'The new Deborah,' says Matilda's biographer, 'perceived that the Lord had sold Sisera into the hands of a woman.' The horrible charges were diligently circulated, with the most disastrous effects upon Henry's reputation in Germany and Italy.

In the summer of 1094, Urban left Rome for Tuscany. From Pisa, where he spent several months, he issued citations to a great synod to be held at Piacenza in the following Lent. Early in February he crossed the Apennines and joined the great countess, who conducted him with immense pomp to Piacenza. So vast was the multitude which came to the synod—30,000 laity, and 4,000 clergy, chiefly from Italy and Gaul—that it could not be contained in any church,

Synod at Piacenza, 1095

and the assembly was held in the plain outside the city.

The old ordinances against simony and clerical marriage were renewed by the synod; the eucharistic question, which had slumbered for some time, was revived, and the doctrine of Berengar was again condemned. But these matters were the least important business of the synod. The empress appeared, and did not shrink from repeating in public the foul and revolting tales which she had told to Matilda and other friends in private. No attempt seems to have been made to test the truth of her statements; a thrill of indignation and disgust convulsed the audience, and Henry was condemned unheard and undefended. Not less momentous was the appearance of the ambassadors sent by the Eastern emperor, Alexius, appealing for help to defend his dominions against the Seljuk Turks. Urban, like Gregory, cherished the hope of reuniting the two branches of the Catholic Church under the supremacy of the Roman see. The call of Gregory to the faithful had fallen upon dull and unheeding ears, but he had not enjoyed Urban's opportunity of advocating the cause in the face of a vast congregation; the eloquent exhortations of Urban, seconded by the presence of the ambassadors, kindled a glow of enthusiasm, and in the acclamations which followed the conclusion of his speech we hear the prelude of that mighty shout which was soon to herald the birth of the first crusade.

Urban remained in Piacenza to the beginning of April, and then proceeded to Cremona, where he was received with great show of reverence by Conrad. The rebel against his own father figured as the obedient son of the Church, humbly held the bridle of the pope's mule as he entered the town, and took an oath to defend the person of the pope and the property of the see. The pope in his turn promised to aid Conrad to win and keep his kingdom, and to crown him emperor when he should visit Rome; saving always the rights of the Church, and especially those touching investiture. The subjection of Conrad to the papal party was completed by his betrothal to the infant daughter of count Roger of Sicily.

Urban's progress through Lombardy and Burgundy

The revolt of his son and the accusations of his wife had shattered Henry's power in Italy. From Lombardy to Apulia the authority of Urban was unquestionably dominant. But the most signal display of his power was to be made in the land of his birth. After paying a visit to Milan, where he was received with enthusiasm, he set forth for Burgundy. On August 1 he crossed the Alps; on the 5th he was in Valence, on the 15th at Puy and Velay. Here summonses were issued for a great council to be held at Clermont, in Auvergne, on November 18th, and the interval was spent in making a progress through Burgundy, consecrating churches, arbitrating in disputes, and dispensing privileges. At Clugny he was naturally received with peculiar honour, and here, on October 25, he consecrated the high altar of the great church which was still in course of building.

The day appointed for the council arrived; the diligence with which the citations had been circulated, the reputation of the pope, and the expectation that he would repeat the call to the faithful to take up arms against the infidel, brought together an extraordinary multitude. Thirteen archbishops, eighty bishops, and ninety abbots attended; the crowd of clergy, monks, and laymen was countless. Yet it could not fairly be called a general council, for there were no representative men from Germany. and only one from England. The first seven days were occupied in reiterating the old decrees against simony, clerical marriage, in forbidding investiture by laymen, and in framing definite rules for observing the 'Truce of God,' a custom which now received the formal sanction of the Church. Philip I. was excommunicated for his adulterous connexion with Bertrada, wife of count Fulk of Anjou, but was not deposed, nor were his subjects absolved from their allegiance. But even the excommunication of the king of France seemed a matter of small importance compared with the great act which was reserved for the conclusion of the session. On November 26, the ninth day after the opening of the council, in a broad space beneath the open sky (for no building could contain the vast concourse), the pope, in a torrent of passionate eloquence, called upon the faithful to come to the rescue of their suffering brethren in the East, and to deliver from the profane hands of the infidel the land which was sanctified by the life, the labours, the death and resurrection of the divine Saviour of men. 'It is the will of God, it is the will of God!' was the answer which burst in one tremendous shout from the enraptured multitude. Such was the birth of the first crusade. It is one of the most astonishing examples of the effect of a single speech uttered by the right man at the right moment. Men had long believed in a peculiar blessing to be gained from visiting the holy places in the East. The

Council of Clermont, November 18, 1095

preaching of Peter the hermit of Picardy, and the tales which he had told of the cruel sufferings of Christians at the hands of the infidel, had lately kindled in thousands of hearts a burning desire to avenge their wrongs and save the most sacred land in the world from desecration. The speech of Urban blew the flame of enthusiasm into a blaze, and being uttered by the vicar of St. Peter, it seemed to come with the force of a command from heaven.

It is not easy for us to realise the reckless and prodigal zeal with which men flung themselves into the crusading movement. But it was an age in which the childlike eagerness, simplicity and directness with which men pursued their ends continually excite our wonder, and often compel our admiration. They were carried along, with little forethought or reflection, on the tide of some bounding emotion, which conducted them sometimes, no doubt, into fearful disasters, which more prudent men would have avoided, but sometimes also to triumphs which more prudent men would neither have attempted nor achieved.

But what was the effect of this proclamation of the crusade upon the existing relations between the pope and the emperor?

When the spiritual head of the Roman Empire proclaimed a war for the defence of the faith, it was the natural duty of the emperor, as the temporal head, to lead the hosts of Christendom upon the enterprise; but Henry was disqualified by excommunication, and this inability tended, of course, to lower him still more in the eyes of the world, and so far to weaken him in his contest with the pope. Thus the same event which raised the pope to the pinnacle of glory, dragged the emperor down to a lower level than he had ever reached before. It may have been some consolation to him that the part which he should have played could not be taken by the other chief sovereigns of Europe. Philip of France, although he broke off his adulterous connexion and was absolved, still lay under the cloud of the Church's censure. The king of England, William the Red, was disqualified from any religious undertaking by his profane indifference to all religion. The kings of Spain were occupied with their own crusade.

Urban spent Christmas at Limoges. Early in the following year (1096) he visited Poictiers, Angers, Le Mans, and Tours, where he held his Lenten synod. In the summer he made a progress amongst the southern towns—Bordeaux, Toulouse, Carcassonne, and Nismes—where another synod was held. Crowds assembled wherever he went, and the fire of enthusiasm for the crusade spread with wild rapidity through all Burgundy and France. In September he returned to Italy; in November he went with the countess Matilda to Lucca, where he met a body of crusaders under Robert of Normandy, Stephen of Blois, and Robert of Flanders on their way to winter in Apulia. Urban committed a consecrated banner to Stephen of Blois, and dismissed the warriors with his blessing. At last he approached Rome; the partisans of the antipope seem to have been completely overawed; Urban was welcomed by a procession of citizens, and all Rome, except the castle of St. Angelo, now submitted to him.

The pope's progress through France and Aquitaine

CHAPTER XV.

CLOSE OF THE PONTIFICATE OF URBAN II. ELECTION OF
PASCAL II. REVOLT OF THE EMPEROR'S SON HENRY.
DEATH OF HENRY IV. 1096–1106.

WHILST the pope had been making his grand progresses, the emperor remained inactive and forlorn in the northeast corner of Italy, sojourning chiefly in Verona and Padua. He had no troops, and but few companions. He begged for succour from Venice and Hungary, but none came from either quarter, and he could not return to Germany because the passes were occupied by the enemy. At length a ray of light was shed upon his darkened path. The marriage of the younger Welf with Matilda had brought no satisfaction to husband or wife. As such, indeed, they had never lived together. The countess had received but little aid from him or his father in the contest with Henry, and they were disgusted to find that her possessions were irrevocably made over to the pope. They now broke off their alliance with her, and reconciled themselves with Henry, on the understanding that the elder Welf was to be reinstated in the duchy of Bavaria. Their reconciliation set free the passes of the Alps, and about Easter (1097) Henry quitted Italy, never to return. He was well received at Regensberg, where he spent Whitsuntide; then he went on to Nürnberg, Wurzburg, and finally Speier, where he held a court. Gradually some of his old friends rallied round him, and in May 1098, at

Henry is reconciled with the Welfs and returns to Germany

THE LAST YEARS OF HENRY IV. 171

Mainz, a diet was held, in which Conrad was deprived
of the right of succession, and his brother Henry,
_{His son} now sixteen years old, was elected heir in his
_{Henry}
_{crowned} stead. The emperor took him to Aachen, where
he was crowned, after taking an oath that he would not
attempt to interfere in the affairs of the kingdom during
his father's lifetime.

For the present there was a lull in the strife between
the pope and the emperor, partly because Henry's
party in Italy was completely vanquished, and partly on
account of the overwhelming excitement of the crusade,
absorbing all other interests. Germany was in a deplorable condition of anarchy; Henry's spirit was much
broken and his authority fatally discredited; such nobles
as returned nominally to their allegiance extorted great
privileges as the price of their obedience; many of the
chapters asserted the right of free election, and set up
bishops in opposition to those who were appointed by
the king, and death soon deprived him of several prelates who had been most faithful to his cause: Conrad
of Utrecht and Herman of Cöln died in 1099; and in
1101 Liemar of Bremen, and Eigilbert of Trier.

The triumph of Urban over Henry and the anti-pope
was almost complete, yet even now his position in Italy
was not thoroughly secure. Although Clement himself
resided for the most part in a fortress near Ferrara, the
castle of St. Angelo was still held by his partisans.
The Normans also continued to cause vexation and
_{Urban's} anxiety. Count Roger would not recognise
_{dealings}
_{with Roger} the authority of the papal legate in Sicily,
_{of Sicily,}
₁₀₉₈ and his aggressive movements in Southern
Italy made the pope tremble for the safety of Benevento.

In 1098, Urban went down to Salerno and made terms with Roger, somewhat humiliating to the dignity of the Papacy. Legates were not to be sent to Sicily without the consent of the count or his successors; and when the pope summoned a general council the count was to select the bishops who should attend it, and to determine their number. Certainly the Normans, if sons of the Church, were wilful and wayward sons; but they were too useful and too strong for the pope to venture upon a quarrel with them, and Urban no doubt regarded the concessions now made to Roger as a necessary price to pay for the safety of Benevento, and the maintenance of his own position in Rome.

From Salerno the pope went to Bari, where in October he held a great synod, attended by 185 bishops. The chief subject of debate was the question between the Western and Eastern Churches respecting the procession of the Holy Ghost. The doctrine of the Western Church had the advantage of an unrivalled champion in the person of the most illustrious scholar and theologian of the age. Anselm, archbishop of Canterbury, had sought refuge from the persecution of the king of England, William the Red, with the pope, whom William refused to recognise. He was the honoured guest of Urban, who flatteringly called him 'the Pope of a second world;' and he now astonished the assembly by the eloquence, learning, and invincible logic with which he handled the difficult subject under discussion. Meanwhile Urban's partisans succeeded at last in capturing the castle of St. Angelo; in November he returned to Rome; Christmas and Easter were celebrated in peace, and in the third week

Synod of Bari, 1098

THE LAST YEARS OF HENRY IV. 173

after Easter a great synod was held in St. Peter's, the call to the crusade was repeated, and thousands responded to it with enthusiasm. Genoa and Pisa fitted out ships for the transport of the warriors, and the archbishop of Pisa himself accompanied the expedition, Some of the crusaders entreated Urban himself to go with them, but the venture was too great; Italy was too unquiet, and the party of the anti-pope, although exhausted, was not extinguished. No pope indeed ever accompanied a crusade; the possibility of defeat, of capture, and of insult was too great a risk to be faced by the spiritual head of Christendom. And as for Urban, though he knew it not, his life was fast drawing to its end. On July 29 he died at Rome, so suddenly that there was not time to give him the viaticum.

Death of Urban, 1099

Urban was the third great pope whose pontificate falls within the period of this narrative. He had the restless zeal and energy of Leo IX. combined with more of worldly wisdom and craft. No pope since Leo had made such long and brilliant progresses in distant parts of his spiritual empire; but while Leo had laboured hand in hand with Henry III. for the reformation of the Church, Urban, like Gregory, had to work in opposition to the emperor; he carried on what Gregory had begun; he completed the humiliation of Henry; he set in motion the crusade which Gregory had designed; that supremacy of the Roman See which Gregory had laboured to establish was now undoubtedly acknowledged by Italy, Gaul, and Spain. These countries all recognised Urban as the only lawful pope, and were all drawn together by the common

Results of his pontificate

bond of the crusading movement which he had instigated and directed. The blot in the pontificate of Urban is the feeble and wavering support which he gave to Anselm in his strife with William the Red. The sad truth must be told. In the words of an English chronicler: 'that overcame Rome which overcometh all the world — gold and silver.' The most illustrious scholar and saint in Europe, who was struggling manfully for the very same principles as those which were professed by Urban, was sacrificed to the venality of the Pope's ministers, which Urban ought to have detected and suppressed, but did not.

On August 31, in the church of S. Clemente the cardinals unanimously elected Cardinal Rainerius as Urban's successor, and he was consecrated the next day in St. Peter's, under the title of Pascal II. Pascal was a native of the little town of Bieda in Tuscany, and had lived in Rome for more than thirty years. Gregory VII. had made him a cardinal, and in his principles he was heartily Gregorian, but experience proved him to be deficient in strength of character and purpose. In a small sphere he had the credit of being a resolute and almost a great man, but the difficulties and responsibilities of high office discovered his weakness.

Rainerius elected pope (Pascal II.) 1099

The beginning, however, of his pontificate was prosperous. Roger of Sicily made him a handsome offering of 1,000 ounces of gold, which he used partly in raising troops to attack Albano, where Clement was now residing, partly in bribing the inhabitants to surrender the place. They were not proof against the temptation; but the anti-pope himself escaped to Sutri,

THE LAST YEARS OF HENRY IV. 175

where he tarried for a time, hoping for succour from the north, which came not; then he retired to Civita Castel-
Death of Clement the anti-pope, September A.D. 1100
lana, where he died in September of the following year. Even his enemies admitted that the anti-pope was a man of great ability and real goodness, worthy of a better cause than that which he had sustained with dignity and courage for nearly fifty years. His partisans chose a successor, who was almost immediately captured by Pascal, and another elected in his place soon shared the same fate: both were banished to monasteries in Apulia.

On July 27, 1101, Conrad died at Florence, full of remorse for his rebellion against his father. He had
Death of Conrad, 1101
been a mere puppet in the hands of Matilda and the pope, but his death seemed to remove the last link which bound Italy and Germany together. Not that Pascal's authority was questioned in Germany, but men troubled themselves little about him there, and few would have exerted themselves to support him except the disciples of the great Abbey of Hirschau, which was a kind of German Clugny. For a time there was a lull in the feuds which had distracted the kingdom. The emperor had proclaimed a peace at the diet of Mainz, and required a solemn oath from the nobles to observe it for four years. As soon as he could re-
Condition of Germany
establish order in the kingdom he proposed to go upon a crusade. Had he gone it is possible that he might have restored some lustre to the imperial crown. But the opportunity never came. The task of enforcing order in his kingdom proved too much for his strength. The more resolutely he tried to curb the lawless and oppressive action of the nobles the

deeper became their hatred and discontent. The murder of count Conrad of Beichlingen by a band of peasants (1103), and of count Sieghard by some court officials in a tumult at Regensberg (1104), furnished a pretext for the rumour that the emperor instigated such deeds of violence, and inflamed the public mind against him.

The strife with the pope was only in abeyance. In a letter to the abbot of Clugny, written soon after the death of the anti-pope, Henry had expressed an earnest desire for reconciliation with Rome; but the action of Pascal cut off all hope of a settlement. He publicly renewed the excommunication of Henry; he secretly fomented rebellion in every direction. Henry found himself entangled in an inextricable network of difficulties: the curse of the Church haunted him, turn which way he would, and blighted all his efforts and plans. Under the shadow of that curse he could not enforce his authority at home, and therefore he could not go on the crusade. Disaffection spread, secret meetings were held, and gradually a plot was formed for deposing the king and putting his son Henry on the throne. The young Henry was a selfish, heartless man, consumed with ambition, and was easily persuaded to think that he might restore the empire to its former glory, if he seized the reins of government before it was too late. He was no more inclined than his father to tolerate the turbulent independence of the nobles, or to submit to the dictation of the pope, but he affected sympathy with both as long as it served his turn. He was, in fact, a master in the art of dissimulation. A dispute between an imperialist and a papal party about the election to the see

<small>Revolt of the emperor's son Henry, 1104</small>

of Magdeburg furnished an opportunity for his revolt. A deputation of the imperialists, on their way to the emperor, had been assaulted and captured by count Dietrich, one of the papal faction. In November the emperor set out from Lüttich with a body of troops, to punish Dietrich; on December 12 he reached Fritslar without suspicion of treachery, and the next morning he learned that young Henry with some of the nobles had deserted the camp in the night. It was a crushing blow. The emperor instantly fell back upon Mainz, while the perfidious son made for Bavaria, where he was cordially welcomed by the disaffected and conducted to Regensberg. He pretended that whilst his father was under the curse of the Church he could not conscientiously live with him, and that, with the approval of the pope, he was ready to undertake the administration of the kingdom. After Christmas an embassy was despatched to Pascal, to ask how far Henry was bound by the oath which he had taken to his father at the time of his coronation. Messengers, meanwhile, arrived from the emperor, imploring his son not to be lured by false friends and flatterers into the sins of perjury and rebellion; but the only reply was that, as long as his father remained excommunicate, Henry could not hold any intercourse with him.

In February his envoys returned from Italy with the answer of the pope. Pascal absolved Henry from his oath, and assured him of final salvation if he would play the part of an upright king and a faithful defender of the Church. By a strange inversion of moral principles the new king's reign of righteousness was to start from an act of treachery and

It is sanctioned by the pope

rebellion: an act which immediately plunged the kingdom once more into all the horrors and miseries of civil war. Bishops and nobles were divided into opposing factions. Ruthard, archbishop of Mainz, who had been banished by the emperor for his cruel treatment of the Jews, was one of the first to join the rebellion, together with many of the Saxon and Thuringian nobles. Henry was invited to Saxony, which, as in the days of Rudolf, became the chief centre of revolt. A diet, largely attended, was held at Goslar, where it was resolved that the Church in Saxony should be purged by the expulsion of all imperialist bishops; a decree which was promptly and mercilessly executed; not only were the living ejected from their sees, but the bodies of the dead were dug up and cast away, and the clergy whom the so-called heretics had ordained were re-ordained by the hands of the orthodox.

On May 20 a large synod was held at Nordhausen. Henry was present and affected extreme humility, refusing to wear the royal robes or to occupy the throne which had been prepared for him. He uttered a prayer for the conversion of his father and shed some hypocritical tears, declaring that, in the course which he was now pursuing, his only motive was a desire for the welfare of the kingdom and the Church, and that as soon as his father was reconciled to the Church he would return to his obedience. The simple people applauded these pious sentiments, and with a loud shout of 'Kyrie Eleison' invoked the blessing of heaven on the young king.

Synod at Nordhausen, 1105.

The history of the next six months is a distressing record of intrigue and strife, of the temporary success of perfidy, and the relentless persecution of a father by his own son. The only redeeming feature is that, although both sides were in arms, they shrank from open war, and no blood was shed.

The emperor retreated for a time into Bohemia, but in October he ventured to move westwards, and about the end of the month arrived at Mainz. The inhabitants were attached to him, and ready to take up arms in his cause; but his spirit was broken, and on the approach of his son he abandoned Mainz and retreated to Cöln. Henry entered Mainz, and a diet was summoned to meet there at Christmas, which the pope's legate was to attend. Under such auspices there could be no doubt what the doom of the emperor would be. Nevertheless he resolved to be present in person. This, however, Henry was anxious to prevent, probably fearing that the sight of his father would excite the sympathy of the assembly. He, therefore, advanced to intercept him. On the banks of the Moselle, not far from Coblenz,

Meeting between the emperor and Henry the father and son had a meeting. The emperor flung himself at Henry's feet, and confessed that he deserved chastisement for his sins, but besought his son not to act as the instrument of divine vengeance. Henry appeared to be deeply moved: again he shed tears (which seem to have been always ready when wanted), entreated forgiveness, and promised to return to his obedience whenever his father should be reconciled to the Church. Meanwhile he proposed that they should disband their armies, each retaining a retinue of 300 knights, and spend their Christmas together at Mainz in peace and good-will. Against the advice of his friends, the emperor dismissed his troops and entrusted himself to his son, who guaranteed his safety on oath, and pledged himself to use every effort at the diet to effect a lasting peace. They started for Mainz. The first night was spent at Bingen, Henry treating the emperor with marks of most profound respect, and the deluded father requiting him with signs of fond affection. In the morning the emperor saw that the castle was surrounded with troops: he was informed by Henry that the archbishop of Mainz had declined to meet him whilst he was under the ban of the Church, and that it would be necessary for him to go to the castle of Böckelheim, where he might spend Christmas in security. The emperor perceived that he had been entrapped; he implored Henry to conduct him to Mainz, but in vain; he was conveyed to Böckelheim, and the castle gates closed upon their prisoner. Here he spent a miserable Christmas. Gebhard of Hirschau, bishop of Speier, was his custodian, but spiritual consolations as well as bodily comforts were denied him; the Eucharist was withheld: 'the Holy Child was born for all sinners,' he pathetically writes in a letter to Hugh, abbot of Clugny, 'but for me alone it seems as if he had not been born.' Unwashen, unshorn, half-starved, the unhappy emperor passed five dreary days pent up in the grim fortress while Henry kept the festival in Mainz with pomp and splendour.

On December 27 the bishop came there to announce that the emperor was willing to abdicate, if life and liberty were granted him. The surrender of the royal insignia was demanded, and after a faint resistance the demand was complied with. On the 31st the emperor was brought to Ingelheim, to make a formal abdication. He was required by the cardinal-legate to confess his offences against Gregory and the Papacy. He begged to be tried before accredited judges; but this boon was refused, and the helpless man had no choice but to confess in the terms which were dictated to him. Even then absolution was denied by the legate; it must be reserved for the pope himself to bestow if he saw fit. His freedom was granted on condition of his renouncing for ever all right to reign, and surrendering all royal castles and possessions. To this also he assented: 'he would willingly resign a burden for which his strength had long been unequal, to retire from the world and attend to the salvation of his soul.' Many were moved to tears at this pitiable spectacle of fallen greatness; but this time the son did not affect to weep. Even when his father fell at his feet, imploring forgiveness, he turned his face away, and hardened his heart. Father and son parted, never to meet again. Henry went to Mainz, and there was consecrated king by the papal legate; the royal insignia were brought from the castle of Hammerstein and the ceremony of coronation, once already performed in Aachen at the bidding of the father whom he had deposed, was now repeated. The new king of course professed the warmest devotion to his 'dear mother,' the Church, and his 'dear father,' the pope; in their defence he had unsheathed the sword, and for them he would wear it until death. An embassy was sent to Rome, to beseech the pope to visit Germany and set the Church in order there. The envoys, however, were all captured and detained at Trent by Count Adalbert.

Bishop Gebhard of Constanz, who travelled by another route, was the only one who actually reached Rome, and brought back a flattering letter from the pope to Henry.

Even in Germany, however, the rebels did not carry everything before them so easily as they had expected. In Elsass especially Henry met with a stout resistance; in an insurrection at Ruvach his troops were worsted and the royal insignia were captured. Nor was the spirit of the emperor utterly crushed, and he still had friends, though mainly belonging to the burgher class. He escaped from Ingelheim to Cöln, where the citizens were moved to pity and indignation by the tale of his wrongs and indignities. From Cöln he wrote a letter to Philip, king of France, relating his misfortunes and imploring aid, and another to his old friend and godfather Hugh, abbot of Clugny, so deeply pathetic that one of the chroniclers remarks, he must be a hard-hearted man who could read it without tears. He tells the abbot that he turns to him as a refuge in his distress, because he believes that through his prayers he has been delivered from many perils. 'Would it were possible for me to see thy angelic countenance, to lay my head upon thy bosom who didst carry me from the font of regeneration, and there, bewailing my sins, recount the story of my multitudinous calamities.' The revolt of his son had put the finishing stroke to his sorrows, and he might well say, in the words of David flying from a son not unlike his own, 'Lord, how are they increased that trouble me! many there be that rise against me.' He then describes in detail all which had befallen him since the outbreak of the rebellion, represents that his

The emperor's letter to Hugh, abbot of Clugny

abdication had been forced from him, beseeches the abbot to plead for him with the pope, and declares that he is ready to offer any satisfaction, saving the honour of his throne, which might be deemed acceptable. Meanwhile to prove his willingness to do penance he made a pilgrimage to the church at Aachen barefoot in the winter's cold. Here also he met with a friendly reception from the people and was lodged in the imperial palace. Otbert, bishop of Lüttich, conducted him to his own city, and exerted himself to procure allies. Duke Henry of Lotharingia became the head of a party to defend the emperor against his son. Aid was sought from Philip of France and count Robert of Flanders; perhaps also from England and Denmark. Young Henry became alarmed; he resolved to try and nip this counter movement in the bud by prompt and bold action; he commanded his father to quit Lüttich, and announced his intention of keeping Easter there. The emperor refused to withdraw, and Henry instantly advanced into Lotharingia. The next four months were spent in fruitless negotiations with his father and an unsuccessful siege of Cöln.

In July sickness broke out amongst the troops. Henry moved to Aachen and sent a message to the emperor intended to be an ultimatum. He gave him the option of holding a diet within eight days at Aachen for decision of the strife, or of an appeal to arms. The emperor replied that if Henry disbanded his army, and the nobles ceased to support his unhallowed rebellion, he would meet them in a diet; otherwise he would submit himself and his cause to the almighty and blessed Trinity, the holy Virgin, and all

the saints.' A divine decree was indeed about to end
the long contest. The emperor's reply had scarcely
reached his son before the tidings came that he was no
more. His illness lasted but a very few days; his friend
the bishop of Lüttich heard his confession, and administered the Eucharist to him. He forgave his enemies,
sent messages of peace to the pope and to his son,
together with his sword and ring, and prayed that his
body might rest by the side of his forefathers in the
great cathedral church of Speier which he had himself
completed on the plan begun by his grandfather.

He died on Sunday, August 7, the anniversary of
his victory over Rudolf at Melrichstadt, twenty-eight
years before. He was only fifty-six years of
age, but the incessant toils and heart-breaking
calamities of his tragical career had worn out a constitution which must have been tough to bear the strain
so long. From his childhood, in fact, he had been a
stranger to anything like lasting prosperity, happiness,
or rest.

Death of Henry IV., 1106

Henry did not pretend to mourn over his father's
death, and the implacable wrath of the Church made
war even with the dead. The bishop of Lüttich was
threatened with excommunication by the legate, because
he had dared to receive the body of the emperor within
the walls of his cathedral. It was taken to an unconsecrated chapel outside the town, where it remained nine
days. Only one poor monk, a stranger on his way
home from Jerusalem, watched by the corpse and sang
dirges over it. Then, at Henry's command, it was
brought back to Lüttich, to be conveyed to Speier. The
emperor's bounty and kindness to the poor had endeared

him to the people of Lüttich; they insisted on carrying the body inside the cathedral; multitudes thronged to clasp and kiss the coffin, and carried away handfuls of the earth on which it had lain, to fertilise their fields. On September 3, the stone sarcophagus with the emperor's remains arrived at Speier; it was conducted by the people and clergy in procession to the cathedral church, and deposited beside the bodies of his father and grandfather. But the bishop, Gebhard, declared that it would be an insult to martyrs and saints if the excommunicated lay in the same grave with the faithful. Once more therefore the corpse was taken up and placed in the unconsecrated chapel of S. Afra, hard by the cathedral church. Here it remained for five years. Just at that time Henry had the pope completely in his power. With much solemn pomp he translated his father's body to the ancestral vault on the anniversary of his death, and celebrated the event by bestowing privileges on the citizens of Speier.

The personal appearance and characteristics of Henry IV. have been described by a contemporary but anonymous biographer. He had a tall and stately figure, a handsome countenance, and a flashing, penetrating eye, which seemed to discern friend from foe at a glance; to the poor, and to the humbler clergy, he was liberal and compassionate; the common people were attracted by his frank and genial manner, but he often repelled men of rank by his haughtiness, and by his sternness terrified his enemies. He liked the society of clever men, was an attentive listener rather than a talker, and could interest himself in the productions of science and art.

<small>Character of Henry IV.</small>

No one who follows the sad history of his life will be disposed to pass a severe judgment on his character. His early experience of treachery naturally rendered him suspicious, but there were many whom he trusted too much, and even to his worst enemies he was not unforgiving. The want of moral training in his youth, when he was in some ways over-indulged, and in others too much restrained, accounts for the passionateness of his temper, and the licentiousness of his habits when he became his own master; but the vile and monstrous accusations made against him by his second wife, however difficult to refute, are no less difficult to believe; at any rate they were not proven. He had not a large or comprehensive mind, but he was quick of apprehension and ready in resource. His aim was a simple one: he strove for no novel rights, but for the maintenance of the old imperial power, such as he believed his father had exercised. But the spirit of independence, both in the reformed Church and amongst the nobles, which had been steadily growing during his minority, was too strong for him. He might, perhaps, have conquered in the struggle if he could have organised and led the lower classes against the nobles, or arrayed the German clergy against Rome. But such a policy, even if there had been no such matchless antagonist as Hildebrand to contend with, would have demanded abilities of a higher order than those which Henry possessed. He was not a statesman, and, although a brave and skilful soldier, he was not a great general. Neither in political nor in military affairs had he any deep-laid or far-sighted schemes. So far as he had a plan at all, it was to oppose the pope by forming

THE LAST YEARS OF HENRY IV.

an anti-papal party in Lombardy, and to weaken the nobles by fostering divisions among them; but for the most part he merely met difficulties as they arose; he was often involved in disasters which a man of a more prudent and calculating mind would have avoided, but he generally extricated himself from them with surprising dexterity, and his indomitable perseverance and untiring activity made it difficult for his enemies to obtain a lasting advantage over him.

CHAPTER XVI.

CONTEST OF HENRY V. WITH THE POPE, TO THE DEATH OF PASCAL II. 1106-18.

THE reign of Henry V. opened with fair prospects. Men of all ranks and parties longed for a season of repose, and for the moment Henry was the centre round which all alike could rally. He was an astute man, who saw his opportunities and resolved to make the most of them. An adept in the art of dissembling, he had behaved himself modestly towards the bishops, submissively towards the nobles, and obsequiously towards the pope as long as it served his turn. But now that he was his own master, his real character—in which avarice, selfishness, and overbearing tyranny were conspicuous qualities—began to betray itself. Peace meant, with him, nothing less than the absolute submission of the German nobility, the commonalty, and the Papacy. He soon found out that in Pascal he had to deal with a man of very different

Character of Henry V. and Pascal II.

metal from Gregory or Urban. Pascal was one of those men who, with fixed principles, have neither the skill to adapt them to circumstances, nor the courage to enforce them in the face of opposition. He made bold speeches which he was compelled to retract, and embarked on bold courses of action from which he was compelled to recede. At his first synod he had taken a strong line, inflicted severe penances on the imperialist bishops, and degraded Ravenna from its metropolitan rank. He was flattered by Henry's specious promises, and accepted his invitation to visit Germany, where he hoped to make a grand display of his authority at a large synod to be held at Augsburg. Presently, being alarmed at hearing that the prohibition of lay investiture would be strenuously resisted by the king and nobles, he changed his mind, and resolved to hold a synod in France. If he could secure the support of the French king and the French clergy, it would give him an advantage, he hoped, in dealing with the German powers.

Late in the autumn he set out from Italy, and spent Christmas at Clugny. Citations were issued for a synod to be held at Troyes in the following May. In the interval envoys from Henry had a conference with Pascal, at Châlons on the Marne. They informed him that the king would resolutely insist upon his right to approve the appointment of bishops, and to invest them with the ring and staff. Pascal flatly refused to acquiesce in this right; it would be a relapse into slavery and a dishonour to the clergy to accept those sacred symbols from the bloodstained hands of laymen. The envoys withdrew muttering threats.

The pope in Gaul, 1106

The Council of Troyes was attended by a large

number of French and Burgundian bishops and clergy, but none from Germany. There was much splendour but little enthusiasm. The old decrees against lay investiture and clerical marriage were repeated; some German bishops were suspended for contumacy in disobeying the summons, or for having received investiture at lay hands, but on Henry himself no threat or punishment was pronounced. The severity of the pope to the bishops excited the anger of the clergy; his leniency towards the king provoked their contempt.

Council of Troyes, May 1107

Henry I., king of England, had lately consented to renounce his right to invest with the ring and staff, but now Anselm feared that he would be encouraged to resume it. Henry of Germany certainly set the decrees against lay investiture utterly at defiance. He cared nothing for the pope or the papal party, except so far as he could make them serve his own interests; and, having used the pope to help him to his throne, he now regarded him merely as an adversary or rival, and watched a favourable moment for putting him under his feet.

For two years there was little or no communication between them. Pascal returned to Italy after the Council of Troyes; Henry was occupied with expeditions into Hungary and Bohemia, which brought him neither gain nor glory; for he had not inherited the military capacity or energy of his father.

In the spring of 1110, at a diet held in Regensberg, he announced his intention of visiting Italy in order to be crowned at Rome, to defend the Church, to recover the lands which had been lost to the empire, and to re-establish law and order. Bruno, archbishop of Trier; Frederick, archbishop of Cöln; and Adalbert, the chancellor, were sent as ambassadors in advance, and met with an encouraging reception from the countess Matilda as well as from the pope.

Henry V. prepares to visit Italy, 1110

After a diet had been held at Speier, in the middle of August, the army marched for Italy; Henry crossed the great St. Bernard with one division, while the other took the pass of the Brenner. The descent of an emperor, or heir of the empire, into Italy with a powerful army at his back was an event which had not been witnessed for a long time, and a special chronicler, a man named David (from the Scotch abbey at Wurzburg), who afterwards became bishop of Bangor, accompanied the expedition. For more than ten years the imperial authority south of the Alps had been in abeyance, save in the marches of Verona and Istria and in the duchy of Spoleto, where the emperor's vice-gerent, Werner. a Swabian, vigorously maintained his rights. Elsewhere both the municipalities and the feudal lords had enlarged their possessions and strengthened their independence. Could Italy now have been united under one strong government it might have defied all invaders. But there was no central authority; the great countess was old and failing in strength, and Pascal was not the man to combine and organise diverse and often jarring elements. He was continually harassed by insurrections in Rome and the Campagna, which could only be suppressed by the precarious aid of the Normans. The northern towns were often at strife with their bishops and the neighbouring nobles, and were too jealous of each other to form a league. Milan was at war with Cremona and Lodi, Pisa with Lucca. Henry indeed announced himself to be coming as the friend of Italy and of the Holy See, but all knew him well enough by this time to be sure that his real aim was absolute dominion. The towns, the nobles, the bishops, the pope, and even the Normans, felt that their independence was menaced. Yet the common fear did not lead to any measures for the common defence.

The imperial army mustered in the Roncaglian fields. The Lombard towns, with the exception of
<small>His progress through Lombardy and Tuscany</small> Milan and Pavia, sent in their submission. The countess Matilda acknowledged Henry's suzerainty, and only begged to be exempted from contributing troops to the imperial forces. In November the army moved southwards from Parma. The season was a very rainy one, and great losses of baggage and horses were incurred in crossing the Apennines. Christmas was spent in Florence. Thence they moved to Arezzo. Envoys were sent to Rome with a friendly letter to the citizens, and an invitation to the pope to attend a conference for the settlement of all questions at issue, to be followed by the coronation of the king. The returning envoys met the king at Aquapendente. They brought encouraging replies from the people and the pope, and the chancellor Adalbert and four knights were now sent forward to confer with Pascal while the army halted at Sutri. The
<small>Conference with the pope. His strange proposal</small> pope was in a dilemma. He could not rely on the Romans or on the Normans to offer any resistance to the king, and yet he dared not concede the right of lay investiture—the very point

for which the Church had been making such a long and gallant struggle. He tried to escape by making a proposal which he must have known to be impracticable. He offered the surrender by the clergy of all property and privileges held under the crown: cities, lordships, rights of holding courts, of coining, and receiving customs and dues, were to be given up, and the clergy were to live henceforth entirely upon their tithes and free-will offerings, on condition that the king renounced the right of investiture. Pope and king were to swear to this contract in St. Peter's, and hostages for its fulfilment were to be given on both sides. It suited the king's immediate purpose very well to affect acquiescence in this preposterous proposal.

On February 11 the royal army arrived at Monte Mario. The coronation was to take place on the morrow, which was Sunday. In the morning the king rode to St. Peter's, followed by a brilliant retinue, and escorted by the guilds of the city with music and banners. At the top of the steps before the entrance he was received by the pope and cardinals. He kissed the foot of the pope, who raised him up, and after saluting each other thrice, they walked hand in hand to the silver gates, where Henry took the customary oath to defend the Church and pope in time of need; but he added the significant declaration that he would confirm to all bishops, abbots, and churches whatever had been granted to them by his predecessors. Thus he designed to throw upon the pope all the odium of the proposed surrender of church property.

<small>Henry V. in Rome, 1111</small>

Two chairs were placed on the porphyry pavement

of the church, where the king and the pope were to swear to the covenant. The pope's oath was very strongly worded; it absolutely condemned all participation in worldly affairs, as irreconcilable with the clerical office; the clergy had become ministers of the court rather than of the altar; the property which they were now to restore to the crown they were never to demand back, under pain of excommunication.

<small>Scene in St. Peter's</small>

The pope can hardly have been surprised at the burst of indignation with which the proposed compact was received, especially as there was a clause which bound the king to leave the patrimony of St. Peter intact. The pope, it was said, provided for his own safety, whilst he scrupled not to spoil the Church. Nobles, as well as bishops, exclaimed that the pope's oath was heretical and intolerable. The king withdrew into a side chamber to confer with some of the objectors. The delay was long, and at last the pope sent a request that the king would come back to finish the proceedings. But some of the German bishops presented themselves before the pope, and solemnly declared that his proposal was considered uncanonical and therefore invalid. Pascal attempted to justify it by quotations from the Bible and the Fathers, but in vain. Nothing but the repudiation of the oath would satisfy the German clergy. The day was drawing to a close. The pope and the cardinals were so closely hemmed in by the German soldiers that they could scarcely get up to the altar to celebrate mass: still less were they able to leave the church. They were in fact prisoners, and at nightfall were taken, closely guarded, to a neighbouring hospital. Many of the clergy were shamefully handled on the way, their silver censers wrenched from their hands, their splendid vestments torn off their backs; some were even stripped of their shoes and stockings. Some cardinals who escaped spread the news through the city; the infuriated people took a wild revenge by murdering such German pilgrims and merchants as they could find in the streets.

Pope and cardinals made prisoners by Henry

Early on Monday morning the mob made a violent attack upon the royalists near St. Peter's. Henry himself led a charge against the assailants, and transfixed five of them with his lance, but fell at last from his horse, wounded in the face. Otto, a Milanese viscount, who lent him his own horse, was seized and literally torn to pieces, and his flesh cast to the dogs. After three days Henry found it prudent to retreat towards Soracte; but he carried off the pope and sixteen cardinals with him, and kept them all close prisoners, although they were treated with respect, and he soon released the bishops of Parma, Piacenza, and Reggio, as he wished to keep on good terms with the countess Matilda. He fixed his camp on the Anio, near Tivoli, whence he could easily keep up communications with Rome, and intercept any army which might approach from the south. From that quarter, however, Henry had nothing to fear, and Pascal nothing to hope. Roger of Sicily had died a few years before, and the other Norman leaders, Robert of Capua, great-nephew of Robert Wiscard, and Roger of Apulia, Robert Wiscard's son, were far too much afraid of insurrection at home to think of attacking Henry, or sending succour to the pope. Meanwhile, Henry's troops ravaged the Roman territory, and the strongest pressure was put upon the pope to induce him to concede the right of investiture, out of pity for the sufferings of the prisoners and the degradation of the Roman Church. And at last Pascal gave way. 'For the peace and freedom of the Church,' he said, 'I am constrained to do what I would not have done to save my own life.' And thus the principle for which his predecessors had striven so long and suffered so much was deliberately surrendered, in return for the immediate release of the pope and the cardinals from captivity, and a promise from Henry that he would henceforth be an obedient son of the Church. The compact was sworn to by the pope and sixteen cardinals, and by Henry, his chancellor Adalbert, and thirteen nobles in the camp. A scribe was despatched to Rome to transfer it to parchment, and on his return the pope and the king signed the document.

Compact between Henry and Pascal

Henry had obtained one great object of his visit to Italy, and as soon as he returned to Rome he hastened to secure the other. On April 14 he was crowned emperor in St. Peter's, but it was a sorry ceremonial, hurried over in secrecy and fear, the gates of the Leonine city being closed lest the presence of a multitude should provoke a tumult. And as soon as he had got his crown Henry quitted Rome with all speed. Having spent Whitsuntide at Verona, and concluded a treaty with Venice, he crossed the Alps in June, and sojourned for a time in Bavaria. On August 7 he translated his father's body [1] with great

Coronation of Henry V. 1111

[1] See above, p. 185.

pomp to the cathedral church of Speier, and on August 15 he invested his confidential counsellor, the chancellor Adalbert, with the archbishopric of Mainz. For the moment the emperor seemed to be master of Italy and of the Church, but the history of the next six years is a record of the gradual loss by Henry of all which he had gained, and the retractation by the pope of all the concessions which he had made.

The Gregorian party was, of course, profoundly indignant at the contract made between Henry and Pascal. They held it to be invalid, because extorted by force. At a full meeting of the cardinals the concession to which the pope had stooped was condemned, and the 'privilege,' as the compact was called, was denounced as being not a 'boon' but a 'bane' (pravilegium non privilegium). In Gaul the feeling seems to have been even stronger than in Italy. A great synod of the Gallican clergy summoned to Anse by the archbishop of Lyons was scarcely restrained by the remonstrances of Ivo, the learned bishop of Chartres, from pronouncing anathema on the pope as well as the emperor.

<small>Compact between Henry and Pascal condemned in Italy and France</small>

On March 18 a synod was held in the Lateran at which eleven archbishops and more than one hundred bishops were present. The recent compact with the emperor was of course the subject of fierce debate. At first Pascal offered to resign the Papacy; then he declared that he would abide by the judgment of the synod. The synod formally cancelled the contract, and confirmed all the old decrees prohibiting lay investiture, while Pascal solemnly retracted his concession, declaring that he condemned all which his

<small>Lateran synod, 1112</small>

predecessors, Urban and Gregory, had condemned, and confirmed all which they confirmed. The decision of the synod was conveyed to Henry by Gerard, bishop of Angoulême. He affected to treat it with contempt, but he soon found that the feeling in the Church at large was too strong to be despised. Guido, archbishop of Vienne, was at the head of a powerful opposition in Gaul, which was openly supported by the young king, Louis VI., and secretly encouraged by the pope. A synod held at Vienne on September 16 denounced lay investiture, suspended anathema over Henry for treachery, perjury, and sacrilege, until he should renounce the practice, and demanded the ratification of these resolutions from the pope, with threats of withdrawing their obedience if he did not comply.

Synod of Vienne, September 16

Pascal wrote a humble letter to Guido, assuring him that the compact with Henry was now void. He was, in fact, as much in the power of the zealots as he had been in the power of the emperor. Henry had crushed the pope, but he could not crush the opinions which Hildebrand had planted in the mind of Christendom. He saw that what he had gained was slipping from his grasp, and he was urged by his friends to return to Italy without delay, and force the pope to stand by the covenant; but at this critical moment he was detained by the outbreak of rebellion in Thuringia and Saxony.

Henry's harsh and oppressive rule had excited deep discontent in Germany, both amongst the clergy and the nobles. They repented that they had helped him to the throne, for if the father had chastised them with whips, the son chastised them with

Revolt in Saxony and Thuringia

scorpions. On slight and arbitrary pretexts the nobles were imprisoned and their castles and treasures confiscated, military fiefs and offices of dignity and trust, both secular and clerical, were bestowed on men of low birth, the servile creatures of the emperor. Adalbert, archbishop of Mainz, so lately Henry's most confidential adviser, became the leader of insurrection. His capture and imprisonment, after more than a year of warfare, paralysed the movement for a time, and in the interval Henry celebrated his marriage with Matilda, daughter of Henry I. of England, amid such pomp as had rarely been witnessed. But the spirit of revolt was too deeply seated and widely spread to be long repressed. Saxony became once more the centre of resistance to the royal authority. During the year 1114 the contest was carried on with doubtful results, but on February 11, 1115, a long and bloody battle was fought at Welfesholze, in which Henry's general was slain and his army utterly routed. This reverse animated the courage of the Gregorian party. Cardinal Kuno, the pope's legate in France, had pronounced anathema on Henry in December at Beauvais. The archbishop of Cöln spread the news of this daring act all over Germany, and exhorted all the bishops to cast off the yoke. On March 28, 1115, Kuno repeated the anathema at Reims; on Easter Monday at Cöln, then in Saxony, and finally at Châlons on the Marne.

These proclamations greatly strengthened the cause of the insurgents by giving it a kind of religious sanction. Castle after castle was taken, town after town joined the revolt, and all the lower Rhine and Westphalia seemed to be lost. Henry saw that some vigorous effort must be made to repair his shattered power. His best chance seemed to lie in making a visit to Italy, to deter the pope, if possible, from ratifying the proceedings of his legate and the insurgents. The death of the great countess Matilda (July 24) had opened a favourable opportunity for asserting his authority in Lombardy. He despatched a conciliatory letter to the pope, and early in February he set out, accompanied only by his wife and a few bishops whom he thought he could trust, to negotiate with Pascal. After a short stay at Venice, where he was received with much splendour by the Doge, he pressed on to the territory of Matilda, and occupied at last the castle of Canossa, which his father, save as a suppliant, had never entered. Contrary to expectation, he treated the towns and nobles with great mildness; special favour was shown to the Pisans, and help given for the completion of their cathedral, because they had lately conquered Majorca and Iviza from the Saracens. Privileges were also bestowed on Mantua, Novara, Turin, and Bologna, where the great teacher of law, Warnerius, seems to have been often employed as an arbitrator or assessor in the imperial courts.

Henry's second visit to Italy, 1116

Meanwhile a great synod had been held in Rome. The Gregorians hoped that the pope would no longer vacillate, but boldly ratify the ban pronounced by his legates on the emperor. But Henry was in Italy; his envoy, the abbot of Clugny, was in Rome; and Pascal shrank from taking the step. He tried to occupy the synod with other matters— a strife between rivals for the see of Milan, a dispute between the bishops of Lucca and Pisa. At last a

Synod in Rome, March 6, 1116

bishop lost patience: 'the pope was trifling with their time; they had not come long distances, and through great perils, to discuss such questions as these, but one in comparison with which all others were insignificant.' There was no escape for him, and at last the pope spoke out. 'What he had done was under the pressure of dire necessity, to purchase the freedom of God's people, but it was an evil deed due to human infirmity; he implored all to pray for his forgiveness, and he condemned lay investiture absolutely and for ever.'

Pascal repudiates the compact with Henry

There was a loud shout of approbation. 'God be thanked!' cried Bruno, the abbot of Monte Cassino, 'that the pope hath, with his own mouth, repudiated that shameful and heretical contract.' 'What!' exclaimed cardinal John of Gaeta, 'so saying thou makest the author of the deed heretical; darest thou call the pope an herĕtic? The contract was a wrong, but not a heresy.' 'Not even a wrong,' cried another, 'since it was done to deliver God's people.' The dispute was waxing hot; but at last the pope, having obtained silence, said, 'Hearken, my brethren; the Church of Rome has crushed all heresies, and never yielded to any, for did not the Lord Himself say to Peter, "I have prayed for thee that thy faith fail not"?' and with these words he put an end to the wrangle. He still assumed, however, a somewhat timid and equivocal attitude, which was far from giving satisfaction to the Gregorian party. He confirmed the utterances of Kuno the legate, and Guido of Vienne, but he would not himself pronounce the ban upon Henry. The emperor, indeed, continued to hope for a reconciliation, especially as difficulties were gathering round the pope in Rome.

On March 30 the city prefect died; the Romans tried to force Pascal to appoint a young son in his father's place; Pascal refused, and a fierce tumult broke out. His friend Peter Leone, with his retainers, made a brave resistance, but at last the pope had to quit Rome, and seek shelter in Albano. Here envoys from Henry had an interview with him, and brought back an encouraging report of his friendly disposition. Still Henry did not go to Rome. He lingered till December in the castles on Matilda's territory, and spent January in the Romagna. But at last he accepted an invitation from the prefect and consuls, and set forth, determined to force the wavering pope to a decision. His approach was welcomed; all the papal fortresses near Rome opened their gates, and the count of Tusculum gave him a friendly greeting.

he quits Rome

On Easter-day he made a solemn entry into Rome, but found that the pope had abandoned it, and gone to Capua. The castle of St. Angelo was in the hands of Peter Leone; the church of St. Peter and the adjacent fortresses were in the hands of the prefect. Henry went to the church, where the cardinals were celebrating the festival. He offered to do penance, if he had wronged the Roman Church. No man dared to stand forth as his accuser, and he then requested that he might be crowned, as the custom was on high festivals. The cardinals refused, but Moritz Burdinus, archbishop of Braga, was less scrupulous: he placed the crown on Henry's head in front of the tomb of St. Gregory. The

Henry enters Rome March 25, 1117

His coronation by the archbishop of Braga

people applauded his act, and conducted the emperor in procession to the Lateran palace. On the next day, in the Capitol, he received the homage of all the chief dignitaries, conferred honours and privileges upon many of them, and admitted the youthful prefect to the rank of noble.

Henry now flattered himself with the hope that pope and cardinals would yield to his demands, but in this he was mistaken. Pascal, in a synod at Benevento, anathematised Burdinus for crowning Henry, despatched Kuno into Germany to foment the strife there, and tried to incite the Normans to make an attack upon Rome. In this he did not succeed; but in June, having heard that Henry had quitted Rome to escape the summer heat, he got a few troops together, and began to move northwards. He was detained at Anagni by severe illness, and it was nearly Christmas before he had rallied sufficiently to resume his journey. Owing to the careless watch kept by the prefect, he got into Rome, and even into the castle of St. Angelo, without opposition. The tidings of his arrival caused some revulsion of feeling in his favour; but he had only a short time to live. On the second day after his return, he was again prostrated by illness, and on January 21 he breathed his last.

Death of Pascal, 1118

The pontificate of Pascal had lasted eighteen years, during which he had been involved in perpetual conflicts and perils—in strife with the emperor, with the Roman nobles, with the German prelates, with the Gregorian party amongst the cardinals, and with the Gallican clergy, more papal than himself. His difficulties were in a great measure the consequence of his own lack of foresight and firmness. In principle he was a severe Gregorian, yet he had exasperated that party, and indeed the whole body of the clergy, first by proposing a spoliation of their property and privileges, and then by surrendering the right of investiture, the very thing for the sake of which he had made this preposterous bargain. He loved Rome, and wished to live there, and repair the havoc made by the sack in Robert Wiscard's time; but he was unable to control the turbulence of the people, or secure the confidence and fidelity of the nobles. He was often compelled to fly for safety to Benevento, and he died at last little better than a prisoner in the castle of St. Angelo.

CHAPTER XVII.

THE PONTIFICATES OF GELASIUS II. AND CALIXTUS II. THE CONCORDAT OF WORMS. END OF THE INVESTITURE STRIFE. 1118–23.

THE hopes of peace for the Church and Empire depended mainly on the character of the man who should be elected to succeed Pascal. Henry's position was most critical. In Italy, indeed, where most of his time was spent in the castles which had belonged to Matilda, his authority was not openly disputed, because it was not very prominently asserted; but on the Rhine, the Main, the Weser, and the Elbe it was set at defiance, and Germany was a scene of deplorable anarchy; infested by bands of robbers, who

Critical position of Henry V.
Miserable condition of Germany

laid waste whole towns and villages, so that in many places the habitations of men were deserted and the houses of God closed. The distress was augmented by physical disturbances—earthquakes, tempests, and floods —which were regarded, of course, by many as a divine retribution for the opposition of the emperor to the rights of the Church.

The cardinals lost no time in making an election. On the day of Pascal's death they secretly assembled in the monastery of S. Maria in Pallara on the Palatine, and unanimously chose cardinal John of Gaeta, the papal chancellor, who reluctantly yielded and took the title of Gelasius II. John of Gaeta elected pope. (Gelasius II.) He immediately experienced the danger of his new position. Cencius Frangipane, probably on account of some personal grudge unknown to us, was enraged at the choice of the cardinals, burst into the conclave, seized Gelasius by the throat, threw him down, trampled upon him, and then dragged him in chains to his own castle. It was soon besieged, however, by an indignant multitude, who rescued the pope and conducted him with great pomp and joy to the Lateran. As Gelasius was only a deacon the consecration was delayed to the ensuing Ember week in the beginning of March. Henry hastened to Rome, hoping to overawe the pope and the cardinals before the consecration took place. But Gelasius warily evaded a meeting by quitting Rome the day on which Henry entered it. He His flight from Rome. descended the Tiber to Porto, and, having narrowly escaped capture by a party of imperialists (he had to leave his boat at night, and was carried on the back of a stout cardinal to the Castle of S. Paolo near Ardea), he finally reached his native place, Gaeta. Here messengers arrived from the emperor, imploring him to return to Rome, promising to protect him at his consecration if he would swear to make a friendly settlement of the questions at issue, and threatening to use force if he would not consent. The pope replied that such grave matters could only be determined in a large synod, which he proposed to hold on October 18 at Milan or Cremona. To make a private contract on oath was inconsistent with his dignity and contrary to all precedent.

The emperor did not at all relish the prospect of a synod, and resorted to the extreme measure of setting up an anti-pope. He held an assembly of the people in St. Peter's and laid the reply of the pope before them. The selection of Milan or Cremona for the synod was represented as a slight to the claims and dignity of Rome, and Warnerius of Bologna ingeniously argued that the election of a pope was invalid without the consent of the emperor. It was then proposed that a fresh election should be made; the name of the archbishop of Braga was submitted, and no other being proposed he was elected by the people, the nobles, a few of the clergy, and three cardinals. He was immediately conducted by Henry to the Lateran, and forthwith consecrated and enthroned with the title of Gregory VIII. Two days afterwards, on March 10, Gelasius, having been ordained priest and bishop, was consecrated at Gaeta.

The archbishop of Braga elected as anti-pope, 1118

Gelasius acted with courage and decision. He wrote to the Romans charging them to abstain from all intercourse with the anti-pope, and on Palm Sunday, April 7, he actually pronounced anathema upon him and

Henry. He obtained promises of support from the young duke William of Apulia, and Robert of Capua, and in May Rome was convulsed with terror by the approach of Robert with an army whilst the emperor was absent reducing some rebel strongholds in the neighbourhood. Many of the people fled panic-stricken, dreading a repetition of the horrors which they had suffered at the hands of Robert Wiscard's troops, but Robert of Capua withdrew from Rome almost as soon as he had entered it: Henry returned, kept Whitsunday there (June 2) and then moved northwards.

Gelasius now ventured to return to Rome : the antipope was feebly supported and presently withdrew to Sutri. The malignity, however, of the Frangipani against Gelasius was still unsatiated. On July 21 Cencius and Leo burst into the Church of S. Prassede, where he was celebrating mass. A fierce scuffle ensued both inside and outside the church. Gelasius was bravely defended by his friends Stefano Normanno and Crescentius, escaped from his assailants, and fled on horseback, accompanied only by his crossbearer, beyond the walls of Rome. The cross-bearer's horse fell and the cross was dropped. Towards evening the pope's friends went out to seek for him and found him in a field near S. Paolo in a pitiable state of exhaustion. They brought him back to Rome, but he now determined to quit it, until happier times should come, quoting our Lord's words, 'When they persecute you in one city, flee unto another.'

After appointing the cardinal-bishop of Porto as his vicar in Rome, and another cardinal as his vicar in Benevento, and commending the defence of Rome to

THE CONCLUSION OF THE STRIFE

Stefano Normanno, he went down the Tiber, with a numerous company, to the sea, where he took ship and in a few days landed at Pisa. Here he consecrated the cathedral church—that miracle of beauty which had been in process of building for fifty years—and confirmed the metropolitan rights which had been bestowed upon the see by Urban II. On October 10 he was at Genoa. Here he embarked again, landed at Marseilles on the 23rd, and thence proceeded to St. Gilles, where he was received with respectful enthusiasm by the abbot of Clugny and a large number of French and Burgundian prelates and nobles. The pontiff, who in Italy had to travel like a hunted fugitive, was conducted on his journey through Burgundy like a triumphant prince.

On January 1 he held a synod at Vienne, and announced another to be held in March. Meanwhile he proposed visiting Clugny, but on the way he was seized with pleurisy, and reached the monastery only to die. Within those peaceful walls he breathed his last, on January 18, after a brief pontificate, lasting less than a year.

Death of Gelasius II. 1119

The death of Gelasius was a check to the progress of the Gregorian party in Germany. Kuno of Palestrina had gone thither as papal legate, and at a great synod, held in Cöln in May 1118, had proclaimed the ban pronounced by the pope on Henry and his adherents. He and Adalbert of Mainz were working vigorously in the papal interest when the emperor returned from Italy, and, by dint of mingled threats, force, promises, and concessions, won back many of the nobles to their obedience. Just when the Church party were looking forward to the synod appointed to be held at

Milan on October 18, they heard that Gelasius was on his way to Burgundy. Kuno then left Germany to join the pope, and the departure of the legate cleared the way for the emperor in his efforts to reassert his own authority.

The dying pope recommended Kuno as his successor, but he declined the onerous and perilous office, and suggested Guido, archbishop of Vienne, as better fitted for it by his high birth, and practical wisdom and experience. Guido was on his way to Clugny when Gelasius died. He was immediately chosen pope by the few cardinals who were present, the choice was confirmed by some of the clergy and laity in Burgundy, and on February 9 he was consecrated at Vienne, under the title of Calixtus II. The election was irregular, but it met with universal approbation, and in Rome it was ratified by the cardinals, the clergy, and the citizens. The new pope was connected with the chief sovereigns in Europe. Louis of France had married his niece; Alphonso, heir to the throne of Castille, was his nephew; the emperor and he had a common ancestress in Agnes of Poictiers; and even Henry of England counted him for a kinsman, as they were both of them great-grandsons of Richard II. (the Good), duke of Normandy. Guido was the first secular priest who had been elected pope since Alexander II.; the Hildebrandine party had naturally been supported mainly by monks, and the vehemence with which they tried to enforce clerical celibacy deepened the ill-feeling which had long existed between the secular and regular clergy. The election of Guido opened a prospect of softening this antagonism, and the lay

Guido of Vienne elected pope (Calixtus II.) 1119

nobles were more willing to pay deference to a pope so royally connected than to a monk of humble and obscure birth. New hopes dawned of bringing the weary strife between the Empire and the Church to a conclusion. The cardinals at Rome expressed an earnest wish to have a synod summoned as soon as possible for a settlement of the questions at issue, and Calixtus issued circular letters intimating his intention of holding one at Reims in the autumn.

All things at last seemed to concur in smoothing the way for peace. Germany was exhausted by internal war and disorder; the emperor gratified the nobles by his gentle and conciliatory demeanour at a large diet which was held on St. John's day at Tribur; most of them returned to their allegiance, and the property taken by each side from the other in the war was restored. Envoys from Rome and Vienna asking for the recognition of Calixtus were favourably received, and although a formal decision was reserved for the synod of Reims, the cause of the anti-pope was quietly abandoned.

On October 1, when Henry was in Strasburg, the abbot of Clugny, and William of Champeaux, the bishop of Châlons, one of the most learned prelates of the age, paid him a visit, and privately discussed the investiture question with him.

<small>Conference with the emperor at Strasburg</small>

They represented that the renunciation of the right would not involve any loss of real power; the kings of France did not invest with the office, yet the French prelates were bound as much as the German to pay taxes, and to render customary services to the sovereign in return for their temporalities. At length the emperor signified his willingness to renounce investiture with the ring and staff, on condition that his authority as feudal suzerain over the prelates was secured. Instructions were given to draw up a contract to this effect, which the emperor solemnly pledged himself to sign at Mouzon on October 24, and the bishops did the like on behalf of the pope.

The council was opened at Reims on October 20. It was the largest and grandest which had been held in that city since the great council in the pontificate of Leo IX., and it was honoured, as that council had not been honoured, by the presence of the king of France. More than two hundred bishops were present, of whom the majority, as was natural, were Gallican, but the archbishop of Mainz, with ten other bishops from Germany, attended. Italy and Spain also were represented; from Normandy came the archbishop of Rouen, and some of his suffragans, and from England came Ralph, archbishop of Canterbury, with three suffragans, and Thurstan of York with two. Thurstan, indeed, had not been consecrated, having refused to make profession of obedience to Canterbury, but he now obtained consecration and the pallium from the pope, much to the indignation of Henry I., who banished him from all his dominions.

Council of Reims, 1119

The pope, surrounded by cardinals and prelates, seated on a lofty platform in the nave of the cathedral church, opened the council with an address, in which, amongst other topics, he referred to the recent negotiations with the emperor. The two prelates then related the course and result of their conference, the abbot of Clugny speaking in Latin, the bishop of Châlons in

THE CONCLUSION OF THE STRIFE 211

French. On the 23rd, the pope, accompanied by cardinals and bishops, set out to meet Henry at Mouzon, a castle belonging to the archbishop of Reims. As they drew near they were informed that the emperor was encamped in the neighbourhood with a large army.

<small>Conference with the emperor at Mouzon.</small>

The friends of the pope became suspicious and alarmed; the terms of the contract were carefully revised, and some obscure passages were amended. Four bishops and the abbot of Clugny then had an interview with Henry and some of his nobles at a manor-house near Mouzon. The revised draft of the contract was submitted to him; he fancied that he detected an artful attempt to deprive him of his feudal rights over ecclesiastics, burst into a rage, and refused to ratify the agreement. Next day the parley was resumed, but without success. The emperor was implacable and obdurate, and the pope rode back to Reims mortified by the failure of his efforts for peace just when he had so nearly grasped it. For two days he was absent from the council, recovering from vexation and fatigue. On the third (October 29) he reappeared, and at this session the old decrees against simony and clerical marriage were confirmed. The draft of a canon was submitted forbidding investiture by laymen with any ecclesiastical office including the temporalities, under penalty of excommunication on those who conferred or received it. But the measure was too strong; both clergy and laity offered a violent opposition to it, and on the following day it was presented in a very much milder form. Investiture with the office of bishop or abbot alone was prohibited, and of church property no mention was made. To the canon thus modified no objections were raised; and thus at last the right lines had been struck out upon which the final settlement of the wearisome strife was to be accomplished. The principle now laid down, that the sacred office could be conveyed only by election and consecration, but that the temporalities might be lawfully bestowed by lay hands, began to take root in men's minds, and the decree of Reims prepared the way for the concordat of Worms.

As yet, however, the emperor was in an attitude of harsh antagonism to the Church; he had not repudiated the anti-pope, and he had contemptuously rejected the last and most strenuous endeavours of the pope to effect peace. Calixtus did not shrink from doing what he conceived to be his duty. On the last day of the council 427 wax tapers were brought into the assembly; the pope solemnly pronounced anathema upon Henry, the anti-pope, and all their adherents; the candles were extinguished and dashed to the ground, after which the pope gave his blessing to the assembly and the Council of Reims was dissolved.

<small>Close of the Council of Reims.</small>

It might seem as if little or nothing had been gained by the council, and as if the rupture between the Papacy and the Empire was as wide as ever; but it was not so. Throughout Germany there was a general desire for peace, and Henry, who had learned wisdom and moderation by experience, made timely concessions to his opponents. He no longer persecuted the adherents of Calixtus, nor did he exact any recognition of the anti-pope.

Calixtus spent the winter in Burgundy, and about the middle of February he set forth for Italy. During April and May he made a progress through Lombardy,

THE CONCLUSION OF THE STRIFE 213

where the chief cities vied with each other in paying him honour. On June 3 he arrived at Rome,
<small>Grand reception of the pope at Rome, June 3, 1120</small> entered the city in state riding upon a white mule, and was conducted by the Frangipani, Stefano Normanno, Peter Leone, and Peter Colonna to the Lateran Palace. After a few weeks he visited Benevento, where he invested William with the duchy of Apulia, and received oaths of fealty from Robert of Capua and other Norman lords. In December he returned to Rome and held an ordination in St. Peter's, which Peter Leone had recovered from the anti-pope. Christmas-day was celebrated in the Lateran Church ; and thus Rome once more had a pontiff who enjoyed undisputed possession of the whole city, and commanded the obedience of all the nobles, the clergy, and the people.

The unhappy anti-pope, abandoned by the power which had set him up, fled to Sutri, where he was feebly supported for a time by Werner, the margrave of Ancona, and Conrad, margrave of Tuscany. He was reduced at last to the shameful expedient of relieving his poverty by the plunder of pilgrims on their way to Rome.

After Easter Sutri was besieged by some papal troops commanded by cardinal John of Crema, and supported
<small>Capture and degradation of the anti-pope, 1121</small> by the presence of the pope himself. In eight days the place was taken, and the so-called Gregory VIII was surrendered into the hands of Calixtus. Clad in coarse buckskin, and mounted on a baggage camel with his face to the tail, which he held as a bridle, the anti-pope was led through the streets of Rome, exposed to the derision and insults of the rabble. After being shifted from one prison to another, he was

made a monk at Cava, where he died, forsaken and forgotten, some years after the death of Calixtus.

The tidings of the pope's successes in Italy were diligently circulated in Germany in order to strengthen the church party there. With the exception of Adalbert of Mainz, who still strove to keep the spirit of revolt alive in Saxony, there was no determined adversary of Henry in his dominions. Bad weather, and famine, the natural consequence of it, and of the wars which had so long desolated the country, made all classes sincerely anxious for peace. Mainz was the only town of importance which (under the influence of the archbishop) still resisted the emperor's authority. Soon after Whitsuntide Henry closely invested it, and Adalbert advanced to its relief with an army raised in Saxony. A battle seemed inevitable; but there was no real heart for fighting on either side. Both the emperor and the nobles shrank from more bloodshed, and it was proposed by them and agreed to by the insurgents that twelve nobles selected from either side should arrange the bases of a settlement to be submitted at Michaelmas to a diet at Wurzburg.

General desire for peace

The assembly at Wurzburg was a very large one. Adalbert and the Saxon nobles dared not approach the town until they had a guarantee of safety; but they were graciously received by Henry himself in front of the city gates. After a session of eight days the emperor and the diet accepted the principal bases of a settlement which were proposed by the committee elected at Mainz; that the investiture question, as being beyond the province of the diet, should be reserved for the decision of a general council to be

Diet of Wurzburg, 1121

held in Germany by the pope, to whose judgment the emperor should then submit; that meanwhile peace should be observed, prisoners and hostages being released, and both sides enjoying their rights and property undisturbed; and that bishops lawfully elected and consecrated should retain their sees until the meeting of the council.

Envoys were despatched to Italy to inform the pope of these resolutions, and early in the year 1122 the bishop of Acqui arrived at Henry's court, bearing a firm, yet conciliatory letter from Calixtus. 'The Church,' he said, 'had no desire to diminish the imperial rights, but only to retain her own. She was not covetous of royal or imperial splendour; only let the Church enjoy what belonged to Christ, and the emperor what belonged to himself. If he hearkened to the apostolic chair, all would be well, but if he lent his ear to flatterers, and neither gave honour to God nor did justice to the Church, the pope, aided by wise and pious men, would provide for the welfare of the Church, not without damage to the emperor.' The letter, we may suppose, was supported by the advice and arguments of the bishop of Acqui, who was a kinsman of the pope and of the emperor, and had already made himself useful to both. At any rate, no objections were raised to the letter, and Bruno, bishop of Speier, and Erlulf, abbot of Fulda, were sent to inform the pope that the emperor and nobles would welcome any settlement which did not inflict injury or humiliation upon the kingdom.

Friendly negotiations between pope and emperor

The pope decided not to cross the Alps himself, but he invested his legate, Lambert, the bishop of Ostia, and the cardinals Saxo and Gregory with full powers to act in his name, and addressed a letter to archbishop Adalbert, expressing his earnest desire to see a peace established, in which the honour of God and of His Church should not suffer.

The legates issued citations to the whole body of the clergy, as well as to dukes, counts, and all faithful laity, to attend the great council to be held on September 8 for the final settlement of the strife between the Church and the Empire. Mainz, the place first selected for the meeting, was abandoned for Worms, this city being in the power of the emperor.

Council at Worms, Sept. 8, 1122

The assembly was a very large one, and the deliberation lasted eight days. At first Henry insisted upon retaining all his rights of investiture, including the presentation of the ring and staff, while Adalbert and the legates maintained no less stiffly that the latter practice must be surrendered. At last a compromise was effected. On condition that the election of prelates should take place in his presence, or in that of his representative, the emperor consented to give up investiture by the ring and staff. The elected prelate was to be invested with the temporalities by the touch of the sceptre, immediately after election, if it took place in Germany, but if elsewhere then within six months after consecration. The declarations of the emperor and the pope, pledging them to the observance of the concordat, were read in the audience of a vast multitude in the plain outside Worms.

The emperor's declaration, which was sealed with the golden seal of the empire, and is still preserved in

THE CONCLUSION OF THE STRIFE

the archives of the Vatican, is to the following effect: 'I Henry, by the grace of God Roman emperor, out of love for God, the holy Roman Church, and the lord Pope Calixtus, do surrender to the holy apostles, Peter and Paul, and the holy Catholic Church, all investiture by ring and staff; and I ordain that in all churches of my realm canonical elections and free consecrations shall take place. The possessions and royal rights of St. Peter whereof he hath been deprived from the beginning of this strife to the present day, either in my father's time or in my own reign, I restore to the holy Roman Church, so far as they are in my power; where they are not, I will honestly help to procure their restoration.' He then promises the like restoration of property which may be due to all other churches, pledges himself to keep peace with the pope and the Roman Church, and to give them assistance and protection whensoever it should be asked. The declaration was signed by eighteen witnesses—nine prelates and nine lay lords—and was sealed by the chancellor, the archbishop of Cöln, whose signature stands in the first line next to that of the archbishop of Mainz.

The Concordat

The original papal declaration has not been preserved, but it was to the effect that the pope conceded to his beloved son Henry, by the grace of God Roman emperor, that in the German kingdom the election of bishops and abbots holding of the empire should be made in the presence of the emperor or his commissioner, free from force or bribery, with an appeal in disputed cases to the metropolitan and bishops of the province. The elected prelate was then to receive all temporalities, save those held directly of the Roman see, by the touch of the sceptre, and was faithfully to discharge all duties thereto pertaining. The pope promises the emperor assistance in all cases where it could be lawfully rendered.

After the declaration had been read, the bishop of Ostia celebrated mass, administered the holy elements to the emperor, and gave him the kiss of peace. Thus Henry was restored to the communion of the Church without any act of penance, or any formal act of absolution. Church and king, pope and emperor were reconciled at last, and the strife was healed which for more than half a century had agitated Christendom, and in Germany had set town against town and class against class, had cost some of the best blood, and reduced the whole country to the extremity of distress.

And this time at least both the principal signatories to the compact were sincere in their intention to abide by it. Adalbert of Mainz, indeed, repeatedly tried to disturb the settlement by making insinuations at Rome against the good faith of the emperor. Nevertheless pope and emperor honestly stood by the terms of the Concordat. The first occasion of acting upon it was on November 11 at Bamberg, where a new abbot of Fulda, having been elected by the chapter, received the temporalities from the emperor by the touch of the sceptre.

Two of the legates remained in Germany, for the most part at the court, to the end of January (1123), while cardinal Gregory went to Rome to announce the result of the council, accompanied by German envoys, who were the bearers of a letter and gifts from Henry to the pope. The messengers brought back a most friendly reply from Calixtus, expressing his joy at the restoration of the emperor to the bosom of the Church, beseeching him also to reflect upon the mischief done throughout Europe to the faithful by the late prolonged schism, and the vast advantages to be derived from the restoration of peace.

It was a proud and happy day for Calixtus when he presided over the largest general council which had ever assembled in the Lateran, attended by more than three hundred bishops, and nearly a thousand other representatves, clerical and lay, by whom the Concordat of Worms was ratified with acclamation. The authority of Calixtus was respected in Italy as much as in Germany, and during the brief remainder of his pontificate unwonted tranquillity was enjoyed in Rome. The pilgrims were protected, the nobles were induced to build churches instead of fortresses, the towers of the Frangipani were levelled, St. Peter's was repaired, and the traces of the sack by the Normans were as far as possible effaced.

<small>Concordat ratified at Rome</small>

The ideal for which Hildebrand strove—the complete subjugation of the temporal to the spiritual power—had not been accomplished. Nevertheless, the long struggle which he began with the Empire had ended in a substantial triumph for the Church. The Papacy, having successfully grappled with the might of the Franconian emperors, was now prepared to conquer in the more deadly contest which was yet to come with the mightier house of the Hohenstaufen. It had been originally, indeed, reformed by German emperors, but they had in so doing forged a weapon which was to be turned with fatal effect against their successors. With

<small>Results of the strife</small>

Henry III. the days had passed away when men could look to the emperor as the leader with the pope—perhaps rather than the pope—of all religious movements. The great moral reforms, the suppression of simony and of clerical marriage, had been effected by the popes with little or no aid from the Empire, and in the strife of investiture the emperors had been their principal antagonists. The emperors could no longer nominate to the Papacy, but the popes could exercise a potent influence upon elections to the imperial throne, and could bestow or withhold the imperial crown. They could do more: their right to excommunicate the emperor, and all smaller sovereigns, and thus virtually to release subjects from their allegiance, was now generally recognised; it was to the Papacy that the eyes of the world were turned as the final court of appeal, before which all lawless rulers might be arraigned, and in which the divine principles of justice, righteousness, and mercy might be applied to the decision of all causes. This ideal of the Papacy had been impressed upon the mind of Christendom mainly through the genius of Hildebrand, and men clung to it with such tenacity, in spite of severe shocks and disappointments, that it continued through many ages to be one of the strongest supports, both for good and evil, of the papal power.

INDEX.

AACHEN, Henry IV. crowned at, 41; Henry V. crowned at, 171; visit to, of Henry IV., 183

Acqui, bishop of, envoy from Calixtus to Henry V., 215

Adalbert, archbishop of Bremen, declines the Papacy, 17; his power, 59; his character and aims, 65; height of his power, 69; fall from, 70; partial recovery of, 75; his death, 77

Adalbert, chancellor of Henry V., made archbishop of Mainz, 196; becomes leader of sedition, 197, 214; at Council of Worms, 216; tries to upset the concordat, 218

Adelheid of Susa, mother-in-law of Henry IV., 40, 127

Ælfwine, abbot of Ramsey, 30

Agnes of Poictiers, mother of Henry IV., 17, 56, 59, 60, 61, 96, 99, 117, 140

Alberada, first wife of Robert Wiscard, 81

Alexander II. Anselm of Baggio, early life of, 49, 50, 55; elected pope, *ib.*; contest with rival pope, 57, 58, 66; supported by Council of Augsburg, 62–64; death of, 89

Alexius, Eastern emperor, helps Henry IV., 148; invokes aid against the Turks, 165

Altman, bishop of Passau, 145

Altwin, bishop of Brixen, 121

Anno, archbishop of Cöln, opposes Nicolas II., 53; strife of with the Palsgrave Henry, 60; his plot to seize the young king, 60, 61; his character and aims, 64, 65; founds monastery, 71; humiliation of at Rome, 75; death of, 115

Anse, synod at, 196

Anselm, archbishop of Canterbury, at Council of Bari, 172; neglected by Urban II., 174

Anselm, bishop of Lucca, 133; friend of countess Matilda, 147; recommended for Papacy, 152; dies, 158

Anselm of Baggio. *See* Alexander II.

Apulia, Norman conquest of, 19

Argyros, Greek catapan of Bari, 35, 36

Ariald, a leader of the Patarines, 49, 78

Atto made archbishop of Milan, 79, 80

AUGSBURG

Augsburg, council at, 62
Azzo, marquis of Este, 127

Baldwin of Flanders, revolt of, 39; supports policy of Hildebrand, 51
Bari taken by the Normans, 81; council at, 172
Basel, synod at, elects Cadalus anti-pope, 56
Beatrice, wife of Godfrey, duke of Lotharingia, 38; detained at court of Henry III., 39; death of, 120
Benedict, a converted Jew, friend of Hildebrand, 27
Benedict IX., pope, 14; deposed and restored, *ib.*; sells the Papacy, 15; deposed again, 16
Benedict X., irregular election of, as pope, 44; deposed, 48
Benevento, Lombard duchy of, 3; princes of, excommunicated, 20; surrendered to the pope, 32; tumult in, 34; synod at, 52; Gregory VII. visits, 94, 98; attacked by Robert Wiscard, 96; seized by him, 140
Benzo, bishop of Alba, opponent of Hildebrand, 57
Berengar of Tours, his doctrine condemned, 31, 32; reads a recantation, 48
Bernhard, abbot of St. Victor, Marseilles, a papal legate, 135
Bernhard, cardinal deacon, a papal legate, 135
Bertha, wife of Henry IV., 40, 72, 74
Berthold, duke of Carinthia, 104, 105
Böckelheim, Henry IV. imprisoned at, 180

CENCIUS

Bohemia, affairs of, 85, 86
Bohemund, son of Robert Wiscard, 149, 158
Boleslaw I. and II., dukes of Poland, 84, 85
Boniface, marquis of Tuscany, receives Henry III. at Pavia, 16; in league with rebels in Germany, 23; conducts pope Damasus to Rome, 24
Brixen, assembly at, deposes Gregory VII., and elects anti-pope, 144
Bruno, abbot of Monte Cassino, 200
Bruno, bishop of Toul. *See* Leo IX.

Cadalus, bishop of Parma, elected anti-pope, 56; letter of Peter Damiani to, 57; contest of, with Alexander II., 57, 58, 66, 67; death of, 80
Calixtus II. (Guido), archbishop of Vienne, 197; elected pope, 208; presides at Council of Reims, 210; his conference with Henry V. at Mouzon, 211; excommunicates Henry, 212; his reception in Italy, 213; letter of, to Henry V., 215; assents to Concordat of Worms, 217; presides at Lateran Council, 219
Canossa, Gregory VII. at, 126; description of, 128; penance of Henry IV. at, 129-131; Henry IV. repulsed from, 163; occupied by Henry V., 199
Cencius, a Roman citizen, enemy of Gregory VII., 110
Cencius, prefect of Rome, friend of Gregory VII., 110, 118

INDEX

CENCIUS

Cencius Frangipane attacks Gelasius II., 204
Charles the Great, first visit of, to Italy, 6; crowned emperor at Rome, 7; his government and character, 9
Charles Martel, his aid invoked by pope Gregory III., 4
Childeric III., king of the Franks, deposed, 5
Chur, bishop of, 110
Civitate, Leo IX. defeated at, by the Normans, 35
Clement II. (Suidger), bishop of Bamberg, elected pope, 17; crowns Henry III., *ib.*; his reforms, 18; dies, 23
Clermont, council of, 166
Clugny, monastery of, 13, 22, 26, 166, 207
Cöln, 22, 182, 183. *See* Anno
Compostella, archbishop of, his pretensions condemned, 30, 84
Conrad I., German king, 12
Conrad II., emperor, 13
Conrad, son of Henry IV., 74; defeats Matilda's troops, 161; his revolt, 163; crowned at Monza, 164; disinherited, 171; dies, 175
Constantine, the Great, conversion of, 1; forged donation of, 5
Corbey, abbey of, 70
Crusade projected by Gregory VII., 97-99; proclaimed at Piacenza, 165; at Clermont, 167

Damasus II. (Poppo), bishop of Brixen, elected pope, 23, 24
David, chronicler to Henry V., 190
Dedi, rebellion of, 73; his share in revolt of the Saxons, 103

GELASIUS

Desiderius, Lombard king, defeated by Charles the Great, 6
Desiderius, abbot of Monte Cassino. *See* Victor III.
Dietrich, bishop of Verdun, friend of Henry IV., 124, 144
Drogo, son of Tancred of Hauteville, 19; slain at Benevento, 35
Duduc, bishop of Wells, at Council of Reims, 30
Durazzo, Robert Wiscard at, 149

Eadward the Confessor founds Westminster Abbey, 31, 32
Ealdred, bishop of Worcester, envoy to Rome, 31; gets pallium from the Pope, 54
Ebulo, count of Rouci, 84
Erlembald, a leader of the Patarines, 78, 79, 80; killed, 110
Exarchate of Ravenna, end of the, 3; territory of, given by Pippin to the Papacy, 5

False Decretals, the, 11
Fermo, bishopric of, 111
Florence, 45, 57, 147, 191
Forcheim, diet at, deposes Henry IV., 135, 136
Forged donation, the, of Constantine, 5
Frangipani, the, attack Gelasius II., 206; escort Calixtus II. into Rome, 213; their towers levelled, 219. *See* Cencius
Frederick of Lotharingia. *See* Stephen IX.

Gelasius II. (John of Gaeta), cardinal, 200; elected pope, 204; attacked by Cencius

GERALD

Frangipane, *ib.*; excommunicates Henry V. and antipope, 206; attacked again, *ib.*; quits Rome, 207; consecrates cathedral at Pisa, *ib.*; holds synod at Vienne, *ib.*; dies, *ib.*

Gerald, cardinal, bishop of Ostia, 133, 140

Gerbert, made pope by Otto III., 13. *See* Sylvester II.

Gerstungen, conference at, 104; peace of, 108

Gilbert of Lisieux, 81

Girard, count of Galeria, plunders English envoys, 54; excommunicated, *ib.*; sent to German court, *ib.*

Gisulf of Salerno, 90, 94, 98, 158

Godfrey the elder, duke of Lotharingia, rebellion of, 23; does penance, 29; marries Beatrice of Tuscany, 38; distrusted by Henry III., 39; reconciled to him, 40; goes to Italy, 42; supports election of Nicolas II., 45; checks strife between rival popes, 58; his power in Italy, 68; dies, 75

Godfrey, 'hunchback,' son of the above, duke of Lotharingia, 75, 76, 91, 98, 108, 115, 120

Goslar, palace of, attacked, 106; the anti-king Rudolf visits, 139

Gregory III., pope, asks aid from Charles Martel against the Lombards, 4

Gregory V., pope, 13

Gregory VI. buys the Papacy, 15; deposed, 16; accompanied by Hildebrand to Germany, 20; dies at Cöln, *ib.*

GREGORY

Gregory VII. (Hildebrand), early life of, 20, 21; made chaplain to Gregory VI., 22; goes with him to Germany, *ib.*; visits Clugny, *ib.*; accompanies Leo IX. to Rome, 26; made cardinal subdeacon, 27; abbot of St. Paul's, *ib.*; sent as legate to France, 32; leads a deputation to the German court, 38; procures the election of Nicolas II., 45; his aims, 46; assists in degrading Benedict X., 48; arranges league with Richard of Aversa, *ib.*; made archdeacon, 52; his relations to Alexander II., 57, 58; supports the designs of William the Conqueror on England, 81, 82; elected pope, 90; consecrated, 92; visits South Italy, 94; letter of, to Henry IV., 97; designs a crusade, 97-99; beginning of his strife with Henry IV., 108-113; his life attempted, 113, 114; deposed by Council of Worms, 116, 118; deposes Henry IV., 118; absolves him at Canossa, 131; his difficulties and indecision, 138-141; declares Rudolf of Swabia king, 143; deposed by assembly at Brixen, 144; negotiates with Robert Wiscard, 145; besieged in Rome by Henry IV., 147, 148; rescued by Robert Wiscard, 150; goes to Monte Cassino, *ib.*; dies at Salerno, 153; his character and aims, 153-157

Gregory, bishop of Vercelli, 92, 110, 112

HADRIAN

Hadrian I., pope, asks aid of Charles the Great against the Lombards, 6

Halberstadt, bishop of, 103

Harzburg, the, blockaded, 104; church of, destroyed, 106; castle rebuilt, 108

Henry II., emperor, 13

Henry III., emperor, begins reformation of the Church, 13; visits Italy, 16; crowned at Rome, 17; visits South Italy, 18; takes Gregory VI. to Germany, 20; visits Italy again, 39; dies, 41

Henry IV., emperor, birth of, 33; betrothed to Bertha of Susa, 40; abduction of, 61; his education neglected, 62; ceremony of girding with a sword, 67; his marriage, 72; puts down rebellion of Dedi, 73, and of Otto, 76; disliked by the nobles, 77; letter of, to Gregory VII., 95; meets papal legates at Nuremberg, 96, 97; suppresses the Saxon revolt, 102-108; strife of with Gregory VII., 108-113; deposes Gregory, 116; excommunicated and deposed, 118; suspended by diet of Tribur, 124; escapes from Speier, 125; does penance at Canossa, 129; deposed by diet of Forcheim, 135; contest of, with Rudolf of Swabia, 137-146; visits Italy, 147; crowned by anti-pope, 149; quits Rome, *ib.*; returns to Italy, 161; besieges Mantua, 162; repulsed at Canossa, 163; his son Conrad revolts, *ib.*; his forlorn condition, 170; returns to Germany, 171; revolt of his son Henry, 177; im-

HUGH

prisoned, 180; abdicates, 181; letter of, to Hugh of Clugny, 182; visits Aachen, 183; his death and burial, 184, 185, 195; his character, 185-187

Henry V., emperor, son of Henry IV., crowned heir at Aachen, 171; revolt of, 176-177; crowned king at Mainz, 181; visits Italy, 190; crowned at Rome, 195; buries his father at Speier, 196; marries Matilda of England, 198; excommunicated, *ib.*; visits Italy, 199; Rome, 201; critical position of, 203; sets up anti-pope, 205; conference with, at Strasburg, 209; at Mouzon, 211; assents to Concordat of Worms, 217

Henry I., king of France, tries to hinder the Council of Reims, 29

Henry I., king of England, surrenders investiture with ring and staff, 189; marriage of his daughter to Henry V., 198

Henry, bishop of Augsburg, friend of empress Agnes, 60

Herman, bishop of Bamberg, 74, 75, 96, 101, 109

Herman, bishop of Ramsbury, envoy to Rome, 31

Herman, bishop of Metz, 116, 122

Herman of Luxemburg elected anti-king, 147

Hersfeld, abbey of, 104

Hildebrand. *See* Gregory VII.

Hildersheim, bishop of, 103

Hirschau, abbey of, 88, 137, 175

Hugh, abbot of Clugny, 26, 33, 91, 99, 124, 180, 182

HUGH

Hugh, 'the white,' cardinal, 84, 90, 110, 114, 115
Humbert, cardinal, his treatise on simony, 43
Humphrey, son of Tancred of Hauteville, 35
Hungary, affairs of, 84, 85, 107
Huzman, bishop of Speier, 116, 144

Investiture to sacred offices by laymen, condemned, 43, 101, 142; conceded by Pascal II., 195; condemned at Vienne, 197; by Pascal II., 200; discussion about, at Strasburg, 209; at Mouzon, 211; condemned at Council of Reims, *ib.*; the strife concerning, settled, 216
Irnerius, jurist. *See* Warnerius
Isidore, decretals of, 11
Ivo, bishop of Chartres, 196

Jerome, bishop of Prague, 86
John XII., pope, deposed by Otto I., 12
Jordan of Capua conducts Victor III. to Rome, 159; dies, 162

Kaiserswerth, Henry IV. seized at, 60, 61
Kuno, papal legate, excommunicates Henry V., 198, 207; declines the Papacy, 208

Lambert, bishop of Ostia, papal legate at Council of Worms, 215
Landulf, a leader of the Patarines, 49, 78
Landulf of Benevento excommunicated, 20; expelled, 32

MAINZ

Lanfranc, abbot of Bec, opposes Berengar, 31, 32; archbishop of Canterbury, reproved by Gregory VII., 157; indifference of to claims of rival popes, 160
Lateran, great council at the, 47
Lechfeld, battle of the, 12
Lent Synods, the, at Rome, 88, 89, 100, 101, 117, 140, 141, 196
Leo III., pope, invokes aid of Charles the Great, 6; crowns him at Rome, 7
Leo VIII., pope, appointed by Otto I., 12
Leo IX., early history of, 24, 25; elected pope, 26; his vigorous administration, 27, 28; hallows abbey church at Reims, 29; presides at Council of Reims, 30; at synods in Mainz and Rome, 31; captured by the Normans, 35; dies, 37
Liemar, archbishop of Bremen, 97, 101, 130, 133, 171
Liutprand, Lombard king, 3; defeated by Pippin, 6
Lombards, strife of, with the popes, 3; aid of Charles Martel invoked against, 4; defeated by Pippin the Little, 5; by Charles the Great, 6
Lorsch, abbey of, 70
Louis the Pious, emperor, 10
Lüttich, bishop of, 183; people of, attached to Henry IV., 185

Magdeburg, archbishop, 103, 105
Magnus of Saxony, 103
Mainz, Pippin the Little anointed at, 5; synod at, 31. *See* Adalbert and Siegfried

Malmedy, abbey of, 70
Manasse, archbishop of Reims, 91, 100
Maniakês, George, Saracens defeated by, 19
Mantua, council at, 67; siege of, 162
Marriage of the clergy condemned, 28, 66, 101; remarks upon, 155
Matilda, daughter of Boniface and Beatrice of Tuscany, 39; marries Godfrey of Lotharingia, 75; her greatness, 120, 146, 147; sends succour to the pope, 148, 149; marries Welf of Bavaria, 161; her war with Henry IV., 161-164; decline of, 190; acknowledges Henry V. as suzerain, 191; dies, 199
Melfi, synod at, 51
Melrichstadt, battle of, 141
Michael VII., emperor, asks aid against the Turks, 97; son of marries daughter of Robert Wiscard, 145; deposed, *ib.*
Michael Cerularius, patriarch of Constantinople, 36
Milan, ecclesiastical strife in, 49, 50, 78, 110, 111, 112
Moritz Burdinus, archbishop of Braga, 201; elected antipope, 205; excommunicated, 212; degradation of, 213, 214
Mouzon, conference at, 211

Nicephorus Botaniates usurps imperial throne, 145
Nicolas I., his powerful pontificate, 11
Nicolas II., pontificate of, 45-54
Normans, settlement of, in Apulia, 19; take Leo IX.

prisoner, 35; relations of, to the Papacy, 51, 80, 81

Odilo, abbot of Clugny, 21
Ordulf, duke of Saxony, 59, 103
Osnabrück, bishop of, 103
Otbert, bishop of Lüttich, friend of Henry IV., 183
Otranto, loss of, by the Eastern Empire, 81
Otto I., the Great, defeats the Magyars, 12; crowned emperor at Rome, *ib.*; deposes pope John XII., *ib.*
Otto III. puts Germans in the papal chair, 12
Otto, duke of Bavaria, rebellion of, 76; leader in the Saxon revolt, 103
Otto, bishop of Ostia. See Urban II.

Pascal II., pope, 174; excommunicates Henry IV., 176; sanctions revolt of Henry V., 177; character of, 188, 203; presides at Council of Troyes, 189; receives Henry V. in Rome, 192: made captive by Henry, 194; makes compact with Henry and crowns him, 195; retracts his compact, 200; dies, 202
Patarines, a party of zealots in Milan, 49; proceedings of, 78, 110, 133
Peter Damiani, abbot of Monte Avellana, 43; made bishop of Ostia, *ib.*; denounces irregular election of Benedict X., 45; papal legate at Milan, 49, 50; power of Hildebrand over, 52, 53; letter of, to Cadalus, 57; to

PHILIP

Anno of Cöln, 61; dialogue by, 62; at Council of Mantua, 67; letter of, to Henry IV., 68; legate at Council of Frankfort, 74; dies, 89

Philip I., king of France, 100, 101, 156; excommunicated, 167

Piacenza, great council at, 164

Pibo, bishop of Toul, 121

Pippin the Little made king of the Franks, 5; defeats the Lombards and is made patrician of Rome, *ib.*

Pisa, see of, made archiepiscopal, 207; cathedral of, consecrated, *ib.*

Pisans, Saracens defeated by the, 160, 199

Poppo, bishop of Brixen, *see* Damasus II.

Praxedis, second wife of Henry IV., 164, 165

Ralph, archbishop of Canterbury, at Council of Reims, 210

Ravenna, fall of the exarchate of, 3; strife for precedence of see with Aquileia and Milan, 18. *See* Wibert

Reims, abbey church at, hallowed, 29; councils of, 30, 210

Richard of Aversa, 35; seizes Capua, 48; Hildebrand makes treaty with, *ib.*; takes oath of fealty to the pope, 51; protects Alexander II., 55; treaty of, with Gregory VII., 94; attacks Spoleto, 111

Robert I. of Capua, 194, 206

Robert Wiscard, son of Tancred of Hauteville, at battle of Civitate, 35; count of Apulia and Calabria, 48; friend of Desiderius, abbot of Monte

SAXONY

Cassino, 49; takes oath of fealty to the pope, 51; divorces his wife, 81; conquers Sicily, *ib.*; false report of his death, 93; distrusted by Gregory VII., 94; excommunicated, 96, 101; his son married to daughter of Greek emperor, 99; rejects overtures of Henry IV., 111; seizes Benevento, 140; invested with duchy of Apulia, 145; his Eastern designs, *ib.*; capture and sack of Rome by, 150, 151; accompanies Gregory VII. to Monte Cassino, *ib.*; dies, 157

Roger, brother of Robert Wiscard, conquers Sicily, 81; attacks Benevento, 96; expels Saracens from Sicily, 160; daughter of, betrothed to Conrad, son of Henry IV., 166; negotiation of, with Urban II., 171, 172; offerings of to Pascal II., 174; death of, 194

Roger of Apulia, son of Robert Wiscard, 158, 194

Roland of Parma announces deposition of Gregory VII., 117, 118

Roncaglian fields, diet in the, 110

Rudolf, duke of Swabia, 70, 95, 104, 105; elected antiking, 136; acknowledged by papal legates, 139; by the pope, 143; dies, 146

Ruthard, archbishop of Mainz, rebels against Henry IV., 178

Saale river, battle by the, 146

Sancho the Great, king of Castille and Navarre, 83

Saxony, rebellion of, 96, 102–108

Sicily, conquest of, by Robert Wiscard and Roger, 81

Siegburg, monastery at, founded by Anno of Cöln, 71

Siegfried, archbishop of Mainz, 62; obtains pallium, 71; letter of, to the pope, *ib.*; goes as envoy to Rome, 73; cited to synod there, 74; retires to Clugny, 75; letter of Gregory VII. to, 97; mentioned, 107, 110, 115, 118, 123

Sigelgaita, second wife of Robert Wiscard, 158

Simony, prevalence of, 11, 17; condemned, 28, 30, 43, 66, 101, 159

Solomon, king of Hungary, 85, 107

Speier, Henry IV. in confinement at, 124; escapes from, 125; buried at, 185, 195

Spitihnew, duke of Bohemia, 85

Spoleto, Lombard duchy of, 3, 111; bishopric of, 111, 112

Stephen II., pope, anoints Pippin the Little as king, 5

Stephen IX. (Frederick of Lotharingia) goes as envoy to Constantinople, 36; returns, 39; abbot of Monte Cassino, 42; elected pope, *ib.*; dies at Vallombrosa, 44

Strasburg, conference at, 209

Streu river, battle by the, 141

Suidger, bishop of Bamberg. *See* Clement II.

Sutri, synods at, 16, 45; conference at, 191

Swegen Estrithson, king of Denmark, 86, 91

Sylvester II., pope, 13.

Sylvester III., pope, 14; deposed, 16

Tedald made archbishop of Milan by Henry IV., 111, 112, 115, 142

Thurstan, archbishop of York, at Council of Reims, 210

Tostig, earl of Northumberland, visits Rome, 54

Tribur, diet at, 70, 123, 209

Trier, archbishop of, 30, 115

Truce of God, institution of the, 83, 84, 85, 88

Tusculum, counts of, nominate to the Papacy, 13, 14, 15

Udo, archbishop of Trier, 115, 125, 140

Unstrut river, battles by the, 107, 141

Urban II. (Otto), bishop of Ostia, 152; elected pope, 160; sojourns at Benevento, 161; presides at Council of Piacenza, 164; of Clermont, 167; makes a progress through France, 169; negotiations of, with Roger of Sicily, 171; presides at Council of Bari, 172; dies, 173

Utrecht, bishop of, 116

Victor II., Pope, 39, 42

Victor III. (Desiderius), abbot of Monte Cassino, 49; apostolic vicar in Apulia, 145, 146; recommended for the Papacy, 152; elected, 159; dies, *ib.*

Waimar of Salerno, 19, 34

Warnerius or Irnerius of Bologna, jurist, 199, 205

Welf I., duke of Bavaria, 145

Welf II., son of the above, marries countess Matilda,

WERNER

161 ; is reconciled to Henry IV., 170

Werner, count, friend of Henry IV., 66, 69, 72

Westminster, origin of abbey of, 31, 32

Wibert, of Parma, chancellor, 56 ; archbishop of Ravenna, 91, 114 ; excommunicated, 142 ; elected anti-pope, 144 ; consecrated as Clement III., 149 ; crowns Henry IV. at Rome, *ib.*; resides at Ferrara, 171 ; dies, 175

Wido, archbishop of Reims, 30

Wido, archbishop of Milan, 49, 50, 78, 79

William of Hauteville (Iron-arm), conquests of, in Apulia, 19

William, count of Poictiers, supports Hildebrand, 51

William the Conqueror, his designs on England supported by Hildebrand, 81, 82 ; his aid invoked by Gregory VII., 145 ; letters of Gregory to, 156, 157

William II. (the Red), king of England, 160, 169

William, duke of Apulia, 206

William of Champeaux, bishop of Châlons, 209 ; at Council of Reims, 211

Worms, council at, deposes Gregory VII., 115 ; council at, and Concordat of, 217, 219

Wratislaw, duke of Bohemia, 85

Wulfric, abbot of St. Augustine's, Canterbury, 30

Wurzburg, diet at, 214

ZEITZ

York, archbishops of, 54, 210

Zacharias, pope, sanctions deposition of Childeric III., 5, 123

Zeitz, bishop of, partisan of Henry IV., 103

www.ingramcontent.com/pod-product-compliance
Lightning Source LLC
Chambersburg PA
CBHW070248230426
43664CB00014B/2440